INVESTIGATING
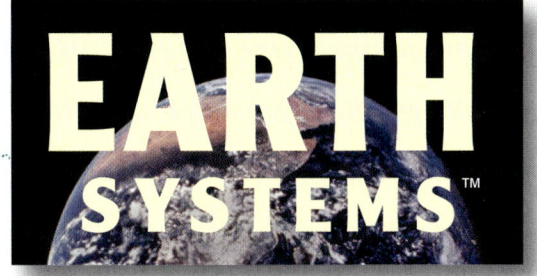

AN INQUIRY EARTH SCIENCE PROGRAM

INVESTIGATING FOSSILS

Michael J. Smith Ph.D.
American Geological Institute

John B. Southard Ph.D.
Massachusetts Institute of Technology

Colin Mably
Curriculum Developer

Developed by the American Geological Institute
Supported by the National Science Foundation and
the American Geological Institute Foundation

Published by
It's About Time, Inc., Armonk, NY

It's About Time, Inc.
84 Business Park Drive, Armonk, NY 10504
Phone (914) 273-2233 Fax (914) 273-2227
1-888-698-TIME (8463)
www.its-about-time.com

President
Laurie Kreindler

Project Editor	**Creative Artwork**	**Senior Photo Consultant**
Ruta Demery	Dennis Falcon	Bruce F. Molnia
Design	**Safety Reviewer**	**Photo Research**
John Nordland	Dr. Edward Robeck	Caitlin Callahan
Production Manager	**Production**	**Contributing Writers**
Joan Lee	Burmar Technical Corporation	William Jones
		Matthew Smith
Studio Manager	**Technical Art**	**Physics Reviewer**
Jon Voss	Armstrong/Burmar	Dr. John Roeder

Illustrations and Photos

Cover photo, courtesy of the Smithsonian Institution; Border photo, Doug Sherman, Geo File Photography
F9, F10, F21, F23, F30, F43, F44, technical art by Burmar Technical
F47 (top photo), Caitlin Callahan; F19, Digital Vision Royalty Free Image (North American Scenics)
F8, James Edmunds; Fvii, Fxiv, F2, F12, F20, F29, F42, F51, F52, F59, illustrations by Dennis Falcon
F54 (diagram modified from "Fossil Horses in Cyberspace") with permission of the Florida Museum of Natural History
Fxiii (upper left), Geological Survey of Western Australia
F35, Bruce S. Grant; F6, Albert M. Hines; F39, Micromass UK LTD
F5, F47, Bruce Molnia; F15, NASA
F26, OAR/National Undersea Research Program; Fxiii (upper right), Fxiv, F17 (top), F28, Paleontological Research Institution
F1, Peabody Museum of Natural History; F36, F48, (photograph montage) F51, F53, PhotoDisc
Fxiii, (lower right), Fxiii (lower left), F4, F17 (top), F25, F32, F37, F58, Doug Sherman, Geo File Photography
F16, F41, F46, F57, Smithsonian Institution
F22 (map), F61 (map), US Geological Survey
F55, Washington State University, College of Veterinary Medicine

All student activities in this textbook have been designed to be as safe as possible, and have been reviewed by professionals specifically for that purpose. As well, appropriate warnings concerning potential safety hazards are included where applicable to particular activities. However, responsibility for safety remains with the student, the classroom teacher, the school principals, and the school board.

Investigating Earth Systems™ is a registered trademark of the American Geological Institute. Registered names and trademarks, etc. used in this publication, even without specific indication thereof, are not to be considered unprotected by law.

It's About Time® is a registered trademark of It's About Time, Inc. Registered names and trademarks, etc. used in this publication, even without specific indication thereof, are not to be considered unprotected by law.

© Copyright 2003: American Geological Institute

All rights reserved. No part of this publication may be reproduced, stored in a retrieval system, or transmitted, in any form or by any means, electronic, mechanical, photocopying, recording, or otherwise, without the prior written permission of the copyright owner.

Care has been taken to trace the ownership of copyright material contained in this publication. The publisher will gladly receive any information that will rectify any reference or credit line in subsequent editions.

Printed and bound in the United States of America

ISBN #1-58591-083-X (Soft Cover)
ISBN #1-58591-107-0 (Hard Cover)

1 2 3 4 5 QC 06 05 04 03 02

This project was supported, in part, by the
National Science Foundation (grant no. 9353035)

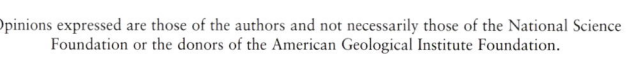

Opinions expressed are those of the authors and not necessarily those of the National Science Foundation or the donors of the American Geological Institute Foundation.

Dedication to Robert L. Heller

The *Investigating Fossils* module of AGI's middle school *Investigating Earth Systems (IES)* program is dedicated to Dr. Robert L. Heller. It was through Bob's vision and determination that the *IES* series was initiated. In 1989, during his tenure as Chair of the AGI Foundation, he initially proposed the need and opportunity for developing a new inquiry-based middle school Earth science curriculum. Working closely with Bill Crain, then Chevron's Corporate Director and Vice President of Worldwide Exploration and Production and a former student of Heller's, they were able to develop support for the curriculum project. Bob and Bill gained the interest of the Chevron Corporation, which graciously provided the seed funding in support of the project. Bob then played a leading role in developing the National Science Foundation proposal to provide the base support for the curriculum project.

Unfortunately, Bob was not able to see the fruits of his labor blossom. In early 1993 Bob was diagnosed with terminal cancer and passed away in July of that year. For all of us who knew and had worked with him, it was a major blow to lose such a close colleague and inspirational educator. It was also a major setback for the curriculum project. Not only did Bob possess the original plan and vision, he had the know-how to ensure appropriate development of the curriculum. I particularly missed not having the opportunity to work under Bob's mentorship in completion of the project. He was a true gentleman, educator, and scientist who brought joy into the lives of us who knew him!

It is particularly fitting that AGI's *Investigating Fossils* module be dedicated in Bob's memory. After teaching, paleontology and stratigraphy were his great passions. He was an expert on the mid-continent lower Paleozoic systems extending across Missouri, Iowa, and Minnesota. He participated in and led many field seminars in the region.

Bob's professional life was devoted to the University of Minnesota in Duluth. He joined the Minnesota faculty in 1950 and established the Geology Department at the Duluth campus. Over the years he advanced from being the only professor of geology on campus to chancellor of the Duluth campus. Bob was passionate about educating young people and in the 1960s served as director of AGI's Earth Science Curriculum Project (ESCP) and later as editor of the first edition of AGI's flagship Earth science textbook. He was President of the National Association of Geology Teachers in 1976 and was President of AGI in 1979. Heller received the Ian Campbell Medal from AGI in 1985 for his vital and significant contributions in education, geoscience research, and science public policy. Additionally, Bob and his wife Geraldine were active in, and supporters of, the cultural and societal affairs of Duluth.

Finally, Bob was family and people oriented. He never showed anger or spoke disrespectfully of anyone. "Forgive everything and remember the best" was an important part of his credo. One of his many remarkable qualities was that whenever he spent time with anyone he would try to ensure that the person left feeling better than when they first met. His friends remember him as strong, vital, wise, unselfish, humble, straightforward, and warm. They called him a leader, an inspiration, a catalyst, a friend, and an eternal optimist.

Bob will be long remembered and sorely missed.

Marcus E. Milling
Executive Director
American Geological Institute

INVESTIGATING FOSSILS

Acknowledgements

Principal Investigator

Michael Smith is Director of Education at the American Geological Institute in Alexandria, Virginia. Dr. Smith worked as an exploration geologist and hydrogeologist. He began his Earth Science teaching career with Shady Side Academy in Pittsburgh, PA in 1988 and most recently taught Earth Science at the Charter School of Wilmington, DE. He earned a doctorate from the University of Pittsburgh's Cognitive Studies in Education Program and joined the faculty of the University of Delaware School of Education in 1995. Dr. Smith received the Outstanding Earth Science Teacher Award for Pennsylvania from the National Association of Geoscience Teachers in 1991, served as Secretary of the National Earth Science Teachers Association, and is a reviewer for Science Education and The Journal of Research in Science Teaching. He worked on the Delaware Teacher Standards, Delaware Science Assessment, National Board of Teacher Certification, and AAAS Project 2061 Curriculum Evaluation programs.

Senior Writer

John Southard received his undergraduate degree from the Massachusetts Institute of Technology in 1960 and his doctorate in geology from Harvard University in 1966. After a National Science Foundation postdoctoral fellowship at the California Institute of Technology, he joined the faculty at the Massachusetts Institute of Technology, where he is currently Professor of Geology emeritus. He was awarded the MIT School of Science teaching prize in 1989 and was one of the first cohorts of first MacVicar Fellows at MIT, in recognition of excellence in undergraduate teaching. He has taught numerous undergraduate courses in introductory geology, sedimentary geology, field geology, and environmental Earth science both at MIT and in Harvard's adult education program. He was editor of the Journal of Sedimentary Petrology from 1992 to 1996, and he continues to do technical editing of scientific books and papers for SEPM, a professional society for sedimentary geology. Dr. Southard received the 2001 Neil Miner Award from the National Association of Geoscience Teachers.

Project Director/Curriculum Designer

Colin Mably has been a key curriculum developer for several NSF-supported national curriculum projects. As learning materials designer to the American Geological Institute, he has directed the design and development of the IES curriculum modules and also training workshops for pilot and field-test teachers.

Project Team

Marcus Milling
Executive Director - AGI, VA

Michael Smith
Principal Investigator - Director of Education - AGI, VA

Colin Mably
Project Director/Curriculum Designer - Educational Visions, MD

Matthew Smith
Project Coordinator
Program Manager - AGI, VA

Fred Finley
Project Evaluator
University of Minnesota, MN

Joe Moran
American Meteorological Society

Lynn Lindow
Pilot Test Evaluator
University of Minnesota, MN

Harvey Rosenbaum
Field Test Evaluator
Montgomery School District, MD

Ann Benbow
Project Advisor - American Chemical Society, DC

Robert Ridky
Original Project Director
University of Maryland, MD

Chip Groat
Original Principal Investigator - University of Texas
El Paso, TX

Marilyn Suiter
Original Co-principal Investigator - AGI, VA

William Houston
Field Test Manager

Caitlin Callahan - Project Assistant

Original and Contributing Authors

Oceans
George Dawson
Florida State University, FL

Joseph F. Donoghue
Florida State University, FL

Ann Benbow
American Chemical Society

Michael Smith
American Geological Institute

Soil
Robert Ridky
University of Maryland, MD

Colin Mably - LaPlata, MD

John Southard
Massachusetts Institute of Technology, MA

Michael Smith
American Geological Institute

Fossils
Robert Gastaldo
Colby College, ME

Colin Mably - LaPlata, MD

Michael Smith
American Geological Institute

Climate and Weather
Mike Mogil
How the Weather Works, MD

Ann Benbow
American Chemical Society

Joe Moran
American Meteorological Society

Michael Smith
American Geological Institute

Energy Resources
Laurie Martin-Vermilyea
American Geological Institute

Michael Smith
American Geological Institute

Dynamic Planet
Michael Smith
American Geological Institute

Rocks and Landforms
Michael Smith
American Geological Institute

Water as a Resource
Ann Benbow
American Chemical Society

Michael Smith
American Geological Institute

Materials and Minerals
Mary Poulton
University of Arizona, AZ

Colin Mably - LaPlata, MD

Michael Smith
American Geological Institute

Advisory Board

Jane Crowder
Middle School Teacher, WA

Kerry Davidson
Louisiana Board of Regents, LA

Joseph D. Exline
Educational Consultant, VA

Louis A. Fernandez
California State University, CA

Frank Watt Ireton
National Earth Science Teachers Association, DC

LeRoy Lee
Wisconsin Academy of Sciences, Arts and Letters, WI

Donald W. Lewis
Chevron Corporation, CA

James V. O'Connor (deceased)
University of the District of Columbia, DC

Roger A. Pielke Sr.
Colorado State University, CO

Dorothy Stout
Cypress College, CA

Lois Veath
Advisory Board Chairperson
Chadron State College, NE

Pilot Test Teachers

Debbie Bambino
Philadelphia, PA

Barbara Barden - Rittman, OH

Louisa Bliss - Bethlehem, NH

Mike Bradshaw - Houston TX

Greta Branch - Reno, NV

Garnetta Chain - Piscataway, NJ

Roy Chambers Portland, OR

Laurie Corbett - Sayre, PA

James Cole - New York, NY

Collette Craig - Reno, NV

Anne Douglas - Houston, TX

Jacqueline Dubin - Roslyn, PA

Jane Evans - Media, PA

Gail Gant - Houston, TX

Joan Gentry - Houston, TX

Pat Gram - Aurora, OH

Robert Haffner - Akron, OH

Joe Hampel - Swarthmore, PA

Wayne Hayes - West Green, GA

Mark Johnson - Reno, NV

Cheryl Joloza - Philadelphia, PA

Jeff Luckey - Houston, TX

Karen Luniewski
Reistertown, MD

Cassie Major - Plainfield, VT

Carol Miller - Houston, TX

Melissa Murray - Reno, NV

Mary-Lou Northrop
North Kingstown, RI

Keith Olive - Ellensburg, WA

Tracey Oliver - Philadelphia, PA

Nicole Pfister - Londonderry, VT

Beth Price - Reno, NV

Joyce Ramig - Houston, TX

Julie Revilla - Woodbridge, VA

Steve Roberts - Meredith, NH

Cheryl Skipworth
Philadelphia, PA

Brent Stenson - Valdosta, GA

Elva Stout - Evans, GA

Regina Toscani
Philadelphia, PA

Bill Waterhouse
North Woodstock, NH

Leonard White
Philadelphia, PA

Paul Williams - Lowerford, VT

Bob Zafran - San Jose, CA

Missi Zender - Twinsburg, OH

Field Test Teachers

Eric Anderson - Carson City, NV

Katie Bauer - Rockport, ME

Kathleen Berdel - Philadelphia, PA

Wanda Blake - Macon, GA

Beverly Bowers
Mannington, WV

Rick Chiera - Monroe Falls, OH

Don Cole - Akron, OH

Patte Cotner - Bossier City, LA

Johnny DeFreese - Haughton, LA

Mary Devine - Astoria, NY

Cheryl Dodes - Queens, NY

Brenda Engstrom - Warwick, RI

Lisa Gioe-Cordi - Brooklyn, NY

Pat Gram - Aurora, OH

Mark Johnson - Reno, NV

Chicory Koren - Kent, OH

Marilyn Krupnick
Philadelphia, PA

Melissa Loftin - Bossier City, LA

Janet Lundy - Reno, NV

Vaughn Martin - Easton, ME

Anita Mathis - Fort Valley, GA

Laurie Newton - Truckee, NV

Debbie O'Gorman - Reno, NV

Joe Parlier - Barnesville, GA

Sunny Posey - Bossier City, LA

Beth Price - Reno, NV

Stan Robinson
Mannington, WV

Mandy Thorne
Mannington, WV

Marti Tomko
Westminster, MD

Jim Trogden - Rittman, OH

Torri Weed - Stonington, ME

Gene Winegart - Shreveport, LA

Dawn Wise - Peru, ME

Paula Wright - Gray, GA

IMPORTANT NOTICE

The *Investigating Earth Systems*™ series of modules is intended for use by students under the direct supervision of a qualified teacher. The experiments described in this book involve substances that may be harmful if they are misused or if the procedures described are not followed. Read cautions carefully and follow all directions. Do not use or combine any substances or materials not specifically called for in carrying out experiments. Other substances are mentioned for educational purposes only and should not be used by students unless the instructions specifically indicate.

The materials, safety information, and procedures contained in this book are believed to be reliable. This information and these procedures should serve only as a starting point for classroom or laboratory practices, and they do not purport to specify minimal legal standards or to represent the policy of the American Geological Institute. No warranty, guarantee, or representation is made by the American Geological Institute as to the accuracy or specificity of the information contained herein, and the American Geological Institute assumes no responsibility in connection therewith. The added safety information is intended to provide basic guidelines for safe practices. It cannot be assumed that all necessary warnings and precautionary measures are contained in the printed material and that other additional information and measures may not be required.

This work is based upon work supported by the National Science Foundation under Grant No. 9353035 with additional support from the Chevron Corporation. Any opinions, findings, and conclusions or recommendations expressed in this publication are those of the authors and do not necessarily reflect the views of the National Science Foundation or the Chevron Corporation. Any mention of trade names does not imply endorsement from the National Science Foundation or the Chevron Corporation.

INVESTIGATING FOSSILS

The American Geological Institute and Investigating Earth Systems

Imagine more than 500,000 Earth scientists worldwide sharing a common voice, and you've just imagined the mission of the American Geological Institute. Our mission is to raise public awareness of the Earth sciences and the role that they play in mankind's use of natural resources, mitigation of natural hazards, and stewardship of the environment. For more than 50 years, AGI has served the scientists and teachers of its Member Societies and hundreds of associated colleges, universities, and corporations by producing Earth science educational materials, *Geotimes*–a geoscience news magazine, GeoRef–a reference database, and government affairs and public awareness programs.

So many important decisions made every day that affect our lives depend upon an understanding of how our Earth works. That's why AGI created *Investigating Earth Systems*. In your *Investigating Earth Systems* classroom, you'll discover the wonder and importance of Earth science. As you investigate minerals, soil, or oceans — do field work in nearby beaches, parks, or streams, explore how fossils form, understand where your energy resources come from, or find out how to forecast weather — you'll gain a better understanding of Earth science and its importance in your life.

We would like to thank the National Science Foundation and the AGI Foundation Members that have been supportive in bringing Earth science to students. The Chevron Corporation provided the initial leadership grant, with additional contributions from the following AGI Foundation Members: Anadarko Petroleum Corp., The Anschutz Foundation, Baker Hughes Foundation, Barrett Resources Corp., Elizabeth and Stephen Bechtel, Jr. Foundation, BPAmoco Foundation, Burlington Resources Foundation, CGG Americas, Inc., Conoco Inc., Consolidated Natural Gas Foundation, Diamond Offshore Co., Dominion Exploration & Production, Inc., EEX Corp., ExxonMobil Foundation, Global Marine Drilling Co., Halliburton Foundation, Inc., Kerr McGee Foundation, Maxus Energy Corp., Noble Drilling Corp., Occidental Petroleum Charitable Foundation, Parker Drilling Co., Phillips Petroleum Co., Santa Fe Snyder Corp., Schlumberger Foundation, Shell Oil Company Foundation, Southwestern Energy Co., Texaco, Inc., Texas Crude Energy, Inc., Unocal Corp. USX Foundation (Marathon Oil Co.).

We at AGI wish you success in your exploration of the Earth System!

Michael J. Smith
Director of Education, AGI

Marcus E. Milling
Executive Director, AGI

Table of Contents

Introducing Fossils	Fxiii
Why are Fossils Important?	Fxiv
Investigation 1: The Properties of Fossils	F1
Fossilization	F4
Investigation 2: Sediment Size and Fossil Formation	F8
Fossilization and Sediment Size	F14
Investigation 3: Conditions for Fossil Formation	F19
The Likelihood of Fossilization	F25
Investigation 4: Fossils through Geologic Time	F28
Telling Geologic Time	F35
Investigation 5: Comparing Fossils over Time	F41
Fossils through Geologic Time	F46
Investigation 6: Adaptations to a Changing Environment	F49
Adaptations	F53
Investigation 7: Being a Paleontologist	F57
Geologic Maps and Cross Sections	F60
Reflecting	F63
The Big Picture	F64
Glossary	F65

INVESTIGATING FOSSILS

Using Investigating Earth Systems

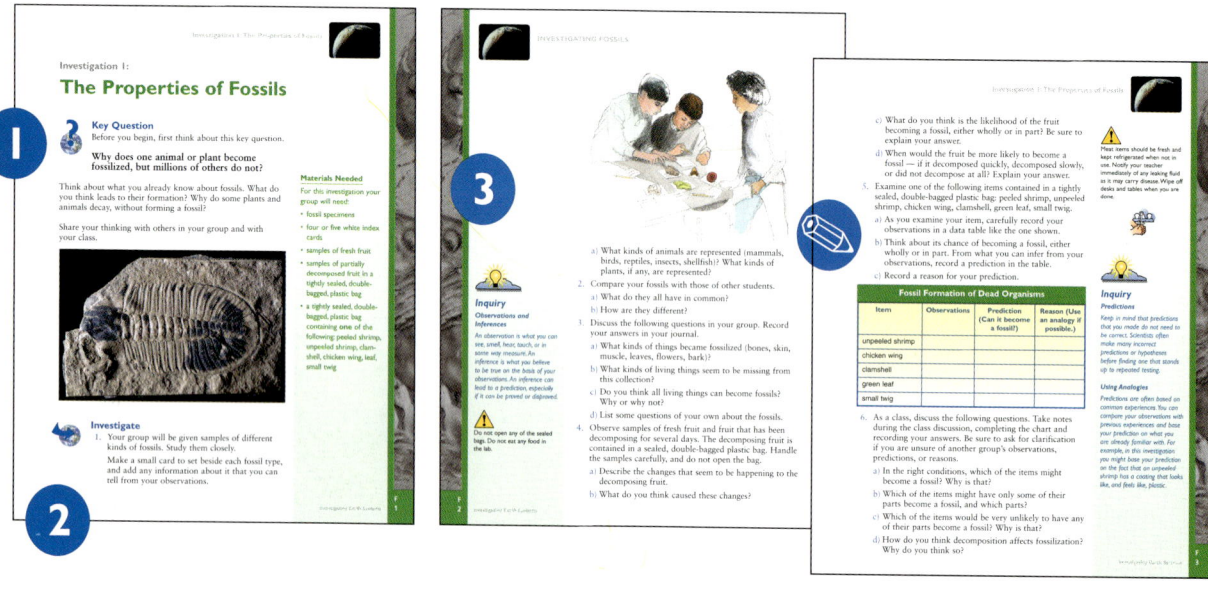

Look for the following features in this module to help you learn about the Earth system.

1. Key Question
Before you begin, you will be asked to think about the key question you will investigate. You do not need to come up with a correct answer. Instead you will be expected to take some time to think about what you already know. You can then share your ideas with your small group and with the class.

2. Investigate
Geoscientists learn about the Earth system by doing investigations. That is exactly what you will be doing. Sometimes you will be given the procedures to follow. Other times you will need to decide what question you want to investigate and what procedure to follow.

3. Inquiry
You will use inquiry processes to investigate and solve problems in an orderly way. Look for these reminders about the processes you are using.

Throughout your investigations you will keep your own journal. Your journal is like one that scientists keep when they investigate a scientific question. You can enter anything you think is important during the investigation. There will also be questions after many of the **Investigate** steps for you to answer and enter in your journal. You will also need to think about how the Earth works as a set of systems. You can write the connections you make after each investigation on your *Earth System Connection* sheet in your journal.

F viii

Investigating Earth Systems

Investigation 1: The Properties of Fossils

Review and Reflect

Review

1. What kinds of plant and animal materials decompose most quickly?
2. What kinds of plant and animal materials take the longest to decompose?
3. What is the difference between a body fossil and a trace fossil?

Reflect

4. What kind of living material has the best chance of becoming a fossil? Explain.
5. Which of the following natural processes did you model in the investigation? Explain your reasoning.
   - decomposition at the Earth's surface
   - scattering of organic matter by scavengers
   - decomposition after an organism is buried by sediments
6. Sediments can often accumulate very quickly in places where rivers flow into the open ocean. Would this be a likely or unlikely place for fossils to form? Explain your answer.

Thinking about the Earth System

7. From what you learned in this investigation, what connections can you make between the geosphere and the biosphere? Note any connections between the two spheres on your *Earth System Connection* sheet.
8. How are the atmosphere and hydrosphere involved in decomposition?
9. On your *Earth System Connection* sheet, note any roles that the atmosphere plays in the preservation of fossils.

Thinking about Scientific Inquiry

10. How is an observation different from an inference? Give an example of each from this investigation.
11. What is an analogy and why is it useful in scientific inquiry? Give an example.

INVESTIGATING FOSSILS

As You Read...
Think about:
1. What is a fossil?
2. Give two examples of a body fossil.
3. Can a plant yield a trace fossil? Why or why not?
4. What are organic compounds made up of?
5. Under what conditions is decomposition the fastest? Under what conditions is it the slowest?
6. What are some ways that animals become fossilized?

Digging Deeper

FOSSILIZATION

What is a Fossil?

A fossil is any evidence of past life. Fossils formed from animal bodies or their imprints are called body fossils. When people think about fossils, they usually think about body fossils. Trace fossils are another kind of fossil. A trace fossil is any evidence of the life activity of an animal that lived in the past. Burrows, tracks, trails, feeding marks, and resting marks are all examples of trace fossils. It is usually hard to figure out exactly which kind of animal made a particular trace fossil. Trace fossils are useful to paleontologists (scientists who study fossils), however, because they tell something about the environment where the animal lived and the animal's behavior.

Investigation 7: Being a Paleontologist

Investigation 7:

Being a Paleontologist

Putting It All Together

Key Question

Before you begin, first think about this key question.

What can fossils tell you about life through time?

Think about what you have learned so far. What kinds of clues can fossils give about Earth history and changing life?

Share your thinking with others in your class. Keep a record of the discussion in your journal.

Materials Needed

For this investigation you will need:
- unknown fossil
- metric ruler and measuring tape
- fossil record charts
- set of known fossil samples
- state or regional geologic map
- access to research material
- materials to create a display

Investigate

1. You will be given an unknown fossil and a geologic map from its state of origin. Examine the fossil carefully.
   a) Write down your first thoughts about it in

F 57

INVESTIGATING FOSSILS

- What kind of rock is it in?
- How old might it be?

Inquiry

Using Maps as Scientific Tools

Scientists collect and review data using tools. You may think of tools as only physical objects like shovels and hand lenses. However, forms in which information is gathered and stored are also tools. In this investigation you are using a geologic map as a scientific tool.

You will have the opportunity to conduct research on your fossil, so that you can compare what you think about it now, to what you think about it later on.

2. Using all of your knowledge and resources about fossils, including your geologic map, find out as much as you can about your fossil.
   Later, you can summarize this to give a "portrait" of your fossil sample. This can be in the form of: a model, a poster, a web page, a magazine article, a newspaper article, a brochure, a diorama, a free-standing display, any other method that you choose.
3. Information that you may be able to find out about your fossil should include:
   - what kind of organism it represents;
   - what the organism looked like when it was alive;
   - what parts of the organism were fossilized and what were not (and why);
   - where the organism might have come from originally;
   - what kind of rock the fossil is in;
   - during what time period the fossil organism lived;

F 58

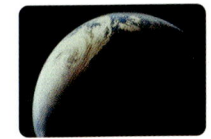

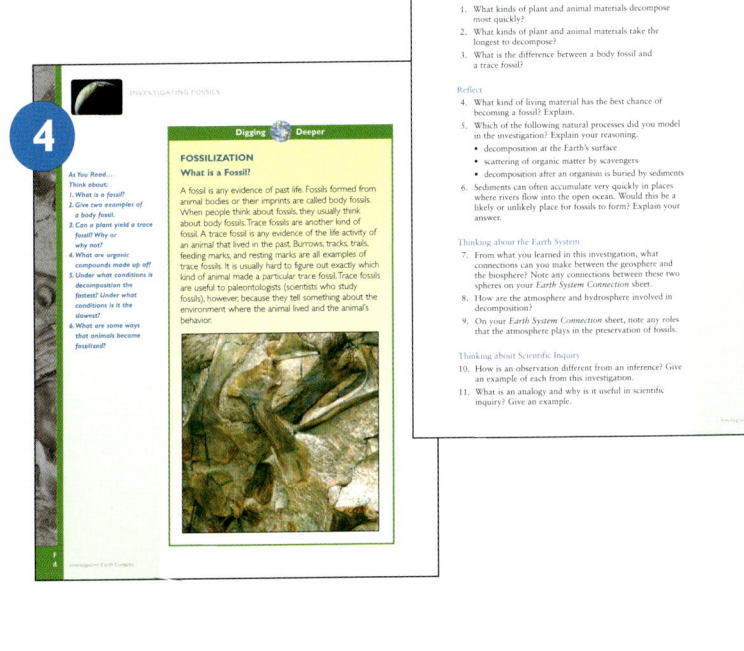

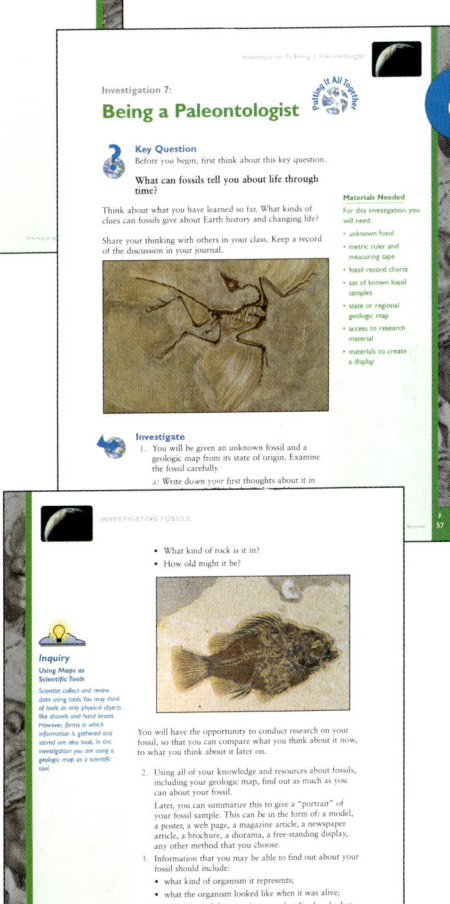

4. Digging Deeper

Scientists build on knowledge that others have discovered through investigation. In this section you can read about the insights scientists have about the question you are investigating. The questions in **As You Read** will help you focus on the information you are looking for.

5. Review and Reflect

After you have completed each investigation, you will be asked to reflect on what you have learned and how it relates to the "Big Picture" of the Earth system. You will also be asked to think about what scientific inquiry processes you used.

6. Investigation: Putting It All Together

In the last investigation of the module you will have a chance to "put it all together." You will be asked to apply all that you have learned in the previous investigations to solve a practical problem. This module is just the beginning! You continue to learn about the Earth system every time you ask questions and make observations about the world around you.

INVESTIGATING FOSSILS

The Earth System

The Earth System is a set of systems that work together in making the world we know. Four of these important systems are:

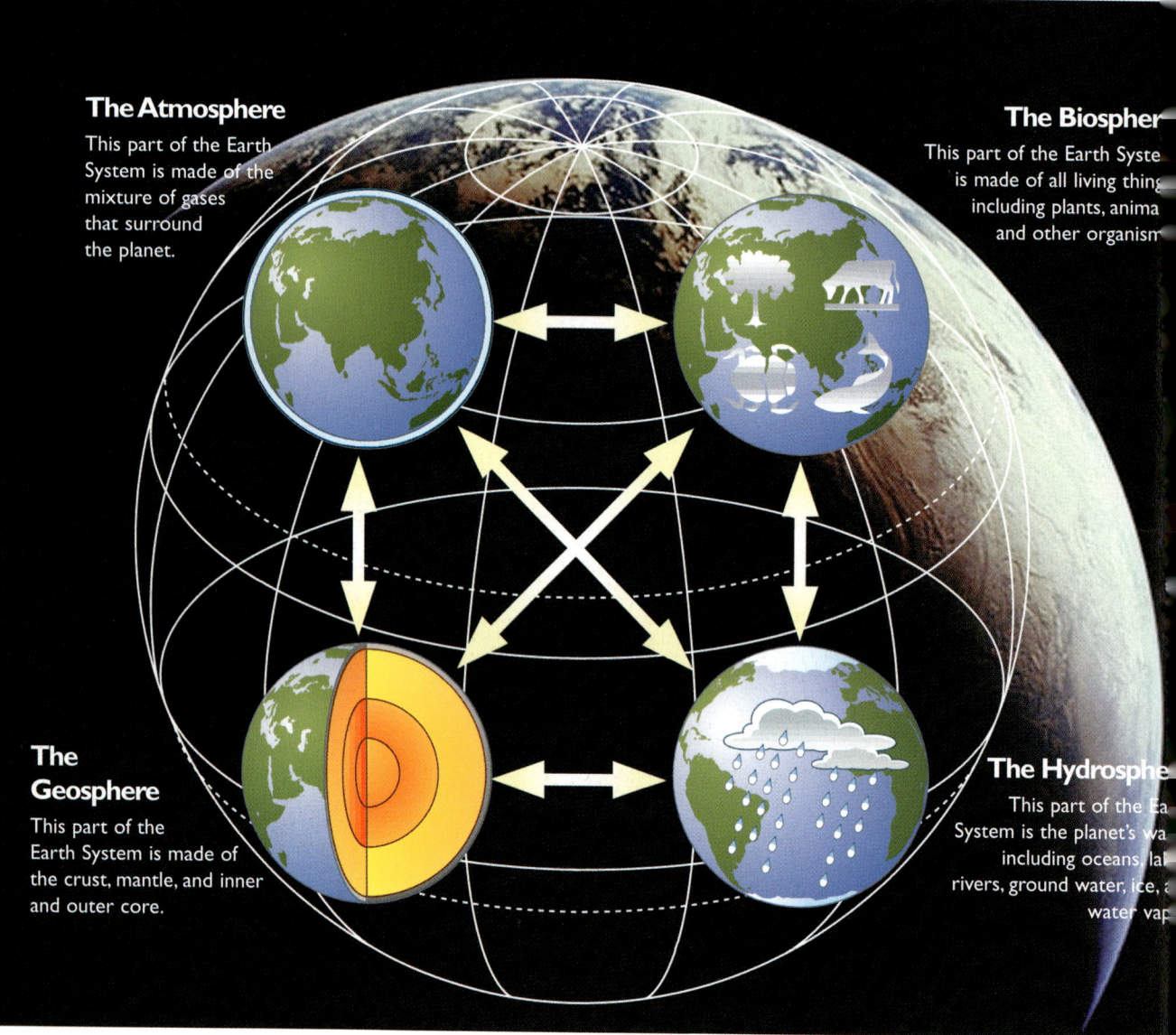

The Atmosphere
This part of the Earth System is made of the mixture of gases that surround the planet.

The Biosphere
This part of the Earth System is made of all living things, including plants, animals, and other organisms.

The Geosphere
This part of the Earth System is made of the crust, mantle, and inner and outer core.

The Hydrosphere
This part of the Earth System is the planet's water, including oceans, lakes, rivers, ground water, ice, and water vapor.

Investigating Earth Systems

These systems, and others, have been working together since the Earth's beginning more than 4.5 billion years ago. They are still working, because the Earth is always changing, even though we cannot always observe these changes. Energy from within and outside the Earth leads to changes in the Earth System. Changes in any one of these systems affects the others. This is why we think of the Earth as made of interrelated systems.

During your investigations, keep the Earth System in mind. At the end of each investigation you will be asked to think about how the things you have discovered fit with the Earth System.

To further understand the Earth System, take a look at **THE BIG PICTURE** shown on page 64.

INVESTIGATING FOSSILS

Introducing Inquiry Processes

When geologists and other scientists investigate the world, they use a set of inquiry processes. Using these processes is very important. They ensure that the research is valid and reliable. In your investigations, you will use these same processes. In this way, you will become a scientist, doing what scientists do. Understanding inquiry processes will help you to investigate questions and solve problems in an orderly way. You will also use inquiry processes in high school, in college, and in your work.

During this module, you will learn when, and how, to use these inquiry processes. Use the chart below as a reference about the inquiry processes.

Inquiry Processes:	How scientists use these processes
Explore questions to answer by inquiry	Scientists usually form a question to investigate after first looking at what is known about a scientific idea. Sometimes they predict the most likely answer to a question. They base this prediction on what they already know or believe to be true.
Design an investigation	To make sure that the way they test ideas is fair, scientists think very carefully about the design of their investigations. They do this to make sure that the results will be valid and reliable.
Conduct an investigation	After scientists have designed an investigation, they conduct their tests. They observe what happens and record the results. Often, they repeat a test several times to ensure reliable results.
Collect and review data using tools	Scientists collect information (data) from their tests. Data can take many forms. Common kinds of data include numerical (numbers), verbal (words), and visual (images). To collect and manage data, scientists use tools such as computers, calculators, tables, charts, and graphs.
Use evidence to develop ideas	Evidence is very important for scientists. Just as in a court case, it is proven evidence that counts. Scientists look at the evidence other scientists have collected, as well as the evidence they have collected themselves.
Consider evidence for explanations	Finding strong evidence does not always provide the complete answer to a scientific question. Scientists look for likely explanations by studying patterns and relationships within the evidence.
Seek alternative explanations	Sometimes, the evidence available is not clear or can be interpreted in other ways. If this is so, scientists look for different ways of explaining the evidence. This may lead to a new idea or question to investigate.
Show evidence & reasons to others	Scientists communicate their findings to other scientists to see if they agree. Other scientists may then try to repeat the investigation to validate the results.
Use mathematics for science inquiry	Scientists use mathematics in their investigations. Accurate measurement, with suitable units is very important for both collecting and analyzing data. Data often consist of numbers and calculations.

Introducing Fossils

Have you ever realized that algae can become fossilized?

Have you ever seen the remains of organisms in rocks?

Have you ever noticed how some rocks are arranged in layers?

Have you ever seen silt that has been washed from the land?

INVESTIGATING FOSSILS

Why Are Fossils Important?

The word fossil comes from the Latin word *fossilis,* meaning "dug up." Today, the word generally refers to any evidence of past life, from insects preserved in amber to imprints of a dinosaur's foot.

To hold a fossil is to hold millions of years of history in the palm of your hand. The ridges, bumps, and curves of a fossilized clam are the same ridges, bumps, and curves that existed as it filtered water from the sea long ago. Studying fossils provides clues about the Earth's past, its climate, natural disasters, changing landforms, and changing oceans. Fossils tell about history and, like all good history, they help you to understand both the present and the future.

What Will You Investigate?

You and your group will be acting as detectives, trying to figure out how fossils form, where they form, and where they might be found today. In this way, you will be doing the work of a paleontologist, a geoscientist who studies life in prehistoric times by using fossil evidence.

Here are some of the things that you will investigate:

- why some things become fossils, but others do not;
- how the environment affects how fossils form;
- how fossils show the age of the Earth;
- how life has changed over time;
- what paleontologists do.

Investigation 1: The Properties of Fossils

Investigation 1:
The Properties of Fossils

Key Question

Before you begin, first think about this key question.

Why does one animal or plant become fossilized, but millions of others do not?

Think about what you already know about fossils. What do you think leads to their formation? Why do some plants and animals decay, without forming a fossil?

Share your thinking with others in your group and with your class.

Materials Needed

For this investigation your group will need:

- fossil specimens
- four or five white index cards
- samples of fresh fruit
- samples of partially decomposed fruit in a tightly sealed, double-bagged, plastic bag
- a tightly sealed, double-bagged, plastic bag containing **one** of the following: peeled shrimp, unpeeled shrimp, clam-shell, chicken wing, leaf, small twig

Investigate

1. Your group will be given samples of different kinds of fossils. Study them closely.

   Make a small card to set beside each fossil type, and add any information about it that you can tell from your observations.

INVESTIGATING FOSSILS

Inquiry

Observations and Inferences

An observation is what you can see, smell, hear, touch, or in some way measure. An inference is what you believe to be true on the basis of your observations. An inference can lead to a prediction, especially if it can be proved or disproved.

Do not open any of the sealed bags. Do not eat any food in the lab.

a) What kinds of animals are represented (mammals, birds, reptiles, insects, shellfish)? What kinds of plants, if any, are represented?

2. Compare your fossils with those of other students.

   a) What do they all have in common?

   b) How are they different?

3. Discuss the following questions in your group. Record your answers in your journal.

   a) What kinds of things became fossilized (bones, skin, muscle, leaves, flowers, bark)?

   b) What kinds of living things seem to be missing from this collection?

   c) Do you think all living things can become fossils? Why or why not?

   d) List some questions of your own about the fossils.

4. Observe samples of fresh fruit and fruit that has been decomposing for several days. The decomposing fruit is contained in a sealed, double-bagged plastic bag. Handle the samples carefully, and do not open the bag.

   a) Describe the changes that seem to be happening to the decomposing fruit.

   b) What do you think caused these changes?

Investigation 1: The Properties of Fossils

c) What do you think is the likelihood of the fruit becoming a fossil, either wholly or in part? Be sure to explain your answer.

d) When would the fruit be more likely to become a fossil — if it decomposed quickly, decomposed slowly, or did not decompose at all? Explain your answer.

5. Examine one of the following items contained in a tightly sealed, double-bagged plastic bag: peeled shrimp, unpeeled shrimp, chicken wing, clamshell, green leaf, small twig.

   a) As you examine your item, carefully record your observations in a data table like the one shown.

   b) Think about its chance of becoming a fossil, either wholly or in part. From what you can infer from your observations, record a prediction in the table.

   c) Record a reason for your prediction.

Meat items should be fresh and kept refrigerated when not in use. Notify your teacher immediately of any leaking fluid, because it may carry disease. Wipe off desks and tables when you are done.

Fossil Formation of Dead Organisms			
Item	Observations	Prediction (Can it become a fossil?)	Reason (Use an analogy if possible.)
unpeeled shrimp			
chicken wing			
clamshell			
green leaf			
small twig			

6. As a class, discuss the following questions. Take notes during the class discussion, completing the chart and recording your answers. Be sure to ask for clarification if you are unsure of another group's observations, predictions, or reasons.

   a) In the right conditions, which of the items might become a fossil? Why is that?

   b) Which of the items might have only some of their parts become a fossil, and which parts?

   c) Which of the items would be very unlikely to have any of their parts become a fossil? Why is that?

   d) How do you think decomposition affects fossilization? Why do you think so?

Inquiry

Predictions

Keep in mind that predictions that you made do not need to be correct. Scientists often make many incorrect predictions or hypotheses before finding one that stands up to repeated testing.

Using Analogies

Predictions are often based on common experiences. You can compare your observations with previous experiences and base your prediction on what you are already familiar with. For example, in this investigation you might base your prediction on the fact that an unpeeled shrimp has a coating that looks like, and feels like, plastic.

Investigating Earth Systems

F
3

INVESTIGATING FOSSILS

As You Read...
Think about:
1. What is a fossil?
2. Give two examples of a body fossil.
3. Can a plant yield a trace fossil? Why or why not?
4. What are organic compounds made up of?
5. Under what conditions is decomposition the fastest? Under what conditions is it the slowest?
6. What are some ways that animals become fossilized?

Digging  Deeper

FOSSILIZATION
What is a Fossil?

A fossil is any evidence of past life. Fossils formed from animal bodies or their imprints are called body fossils. When people think about fossils, they usually think about body fossils. Trace fossils are another kind of fossil. A trace fossil is any evidence of the life activity of an animal that lived in the past. Burrows, tracks, trails, feeding marks, and resting marks are all examples of trace fossils. It is usually hard to figure out exactly which kind of animal made a particular trace fossil. Trace fossils are useful to paleontologists (scientists who study fossils), however, because they tell something about the environment where the animal lived and the animal's behavior.

Investigation 1: The Properties of Fossils

Decomposition

Organisms are made up of chemical compounds, most of which are organic compounds. Organic compounds consist mainly of carbon, oxygen, and hydrogen. After a plant or animal dies, it decomposes. As organisms decompose, their organic compounds change into simpler compounds, mainly carbon dioxide and water. Decomposition is fastest when the organisms are in water that contains dissolved oxygen. Organisms can also decompose even without oxygen. Some kinds of bacteria feed on plant and animal tissues even though there is no oxygen. These are called anaerobic ("no air") bacteria. Sooner or later, almost all organic matter from plants and animals decays. Decay slows down only when the organic matter is buried in very fine mud. That seals the organic matter off from water with oxygen.

The soft parts of an organism decompose the fastest. You know how little time it takes for food to spoil and rot in warm weather when it is not in the refrigerator. Bones and shells decompose much more slowly. Over

INVESTIGATING FOSSILS

long times their mineral materials dissolve. That can happen rapidly when the shells and bones lie on the ground surface or on the sea bottom. If the shell or bone is buried in sediment, it dissolves more slowly. Sometimes the shells are not dissolved before the rock becomes solid, so they are preserved. The woody parts of plants that consist mostly of cellulose and lignin decompose much more slowly than the softer parts.

Fossilization

Most animals become fossilized by being buried in sediment. For them to be fossilized, they have to be buried and leave an imprint before they decompose. Animals without skeletons are seldom fossilized, because they decompose so fast. Animals with hard skeletons are much easier to fossilize. The most common fossils are shells of marine animals like clams, snails, or corals. Insects, with thin outside skeletons of chitin, are not as easy to fossilize. Sometimes an insect is trapped in sticky material, called resin, that comes out of some kinds of trees. Then the resin hardens to a material called amber. The insect fossil is preserved in the amber, often perfectly.

Sometimes the actual shell or bone is preserved. Usually, however, you see only its imprint. If the shell or bone resists being dissolved for a long enough time, the sediment around it turns into rock. Then, even though the shell or bone dissolves, the imprint is preserved. When a hammer splits the rock open, the fracture might pass through the imprint, and you see a fossil.

Investigation 1: The Properties of Fossils

Review and Reflect

Review

1. What kinds of plant and animal materials decompose most quickly?
2. What kinds of plant and animal materials take the longest to decompose?
3. What is the difference between a body fossil and a trace fossil?

Reflect

4. What kinds of materials from organisms have the best chance of becoming a fossil? Explain.
5. Which of the following natural processes did you model in the investigation? Explain your reasoning.
   - decomposition at the Earth's surface
   - scattering of organic matter by scavengers
   - decomposition after an organism is buried by sediments
6. Sediments can often accumulate very quickly in places where rivers flow into the open ocean. Would this be a likely or unlikely place for fossils to form? Explain your answer.

Thinking about the Earth System

7. From what you learned in this investigation, what connections can you make between the geosphere and the biosphere? Note any connections between these two spheres on your *Earth System Connection* sheet.
8. How are the atmosphere and hydrosphere involved in decomposition?
9. On your *Earth System Connection* sheet, note any roles that the atmosphere plays in the preservation of fossils.

Thinking about Scientific Inquiry

10. How is an observation different from an inference? Give an example of each from this investigation.
11. What is an analogy and why is it useful in scientific inquiry? Give an example.

Investigating Earth Systems

F
7

INVESTIGATING FOSSILS

Materials Needed

For this investigation your group will need:

- small amount of each sediment type: clay, fine sand, and coarse sand
- magnifier
- microscope (optional)
- sheet of white paper and black paper
- different-sized spherical objects (i.e., marbles, table-tennis balls, tennis balls, softballs, volleyballs, soccer balls, and basketballs—about three per group)
- metric measuring tape
- calculator (optional)
- newspapers to cover desk
- petroleum jelly
- small container
- plaster (molding plaster or plaster of Paris)
- water supply
- plastic spoon
- leaf, clamshell, and piece of dried fruit

Investigation 2:

Sediment Size and Fossil Formation

Key Question

Before you begin, first think about this key question.

Does sediment size affect how fossils form?

Think about what you know about how a fossil forms. If an animal dies and is buried by gravel, is it as likely to become a body fossil as when it is buried by mud? How might the size of grains of sediment affect whether or not a trace fossil can be formed?

Share your thinking with others in your group and with your class.

Investigate

Part A: Ranking Sediment According to Size

1. In your group, take a close look at samples of three different materials: clay, fine sand, and coarse sand.

Investigation 2: Sediment Size and Fossil Formation

Place a small amount of each of these particles on white paper and also on black paper.

Look at them first with the unaided eye, then with a magnifier, and, if possible, through a microscope. Compare the sizes of grains of sediment for the three samples.

a) Which grains are largest, which are medium-sized, and which are smallest?

b) If you were to compare the sizes of the grains quantitatively (using numbers rather than just ranking them), how many times larger do you think the largest grain is, compared to the medium grain? How many times larger do you think the medium grain is, compared to the smallest grain?

c) If you have access to a microscope with a scale, measure the size of the grains. You may have to measure several grains of each sediment and average the values. Record your results in your journal.

2. Sediment can range in size from large boulders to microscopic flakes of clay. Using a simple analogy, you can get a better idea of how the particle sizes compare with one another.

Obtain at least three different-sized spherical objects. Examples of some objects you can use are given on the following page.

Discuss how you could measure them.

Share your method with other groups and agree on a single method of measurement for the whole class. It is also important to use the same unit of measurement—metric units are highly recommended.

a) Record your method and the units you chose to use in your journal.

Inquiry
Using Measurements

Measurements are important when collecting data. In this investigation your group will need to agree on the measurement units you will use. Consider the United States system of measurement (inches) or metric measurement (millimeters, centimeters). Be sure to have good reasons for what you decide.

Investigating Earth Systems

INVESTIGATING FOSSILS

3. When your group has measured the spheres, share the results. Devise a good way to display the whole class's results, perhaps on a chalkboard, dry-erase board, or overhead transparency sheet.

   a) Did all of the groups use the same method to measure their spheres? Did they use the same units? If not, discuss the different methods and units used and make sure that they all are directly comparable to one another before going any further.

   b) When all groups have contributed their data, create a chart in your journal. Design it like the one shown below (for convenience later on, list the spherical objects in descending order of size). Calculate and record the class's average measurement for each item.

Class Results from Measurements for Sizes of Spheres		
Object	**Class's Average Measurement (include units)**	**Comparison**
basketball		
soccer ball		
volleyball		
softball		
tennis ball		
table-tennis ball		
marble		
other		

4. Choose a way of comparing the sizes (ratio, percent, or other method) and record this in your journal. For example, is a soccer ball 100 times larger than a tennis ball? Five times? Is a table-tennis ball twice the size of a marble? How can you calculate this?

Investigation 2: Sediment Size and Fossil Formation

Discuss the comparison method as a class.

a) When all groups are in agreement, record your comparison for each item. Include all calculations in your journal. If you use a calculator, include the setup for your calculations.

5. Copy the chart shown below into your journal:

Size of Different Sediment Types

Sediment Type	Size Range (particle diameter)	Comparison
Very Coarse Sand	1.0–2.0 mm	
Coarse Sand	0.5–1.0 mm	
Medium Sand	0.25–0.50 mm	
Fine Sand	0.125–0.250 mm	
Very Fine Sand	0.0625–0.1250 mm	
Silt	0.0040–0.0625 mm	
Clay	< 0.004 mm	

Using the same comparison method, compare the sediment types in the chart. Because the values are given as a *range*, not an average, you may want to use the largest (or smallest) value in the range to compare.

a) Record your size comparisons in your journal.

b) Which four spherical objects best represent the relative sizes of the four sediment grains?

6. Discuss your group's results with the rest of the class.

a) Explain your comparisons mathematically. How did you arrive at your numbers?

b) Did your group do anything different, compared to other groups? Explain.

Inquiry
Using Mathematics

Using mathematics as a tool helps scientists to be more precise about the observations they make. Data often consists of numbers and calculations. In this investigation you used calculations to make size comparisons.

Part B: Sediment Grain Size and Fossilization

1. Suppose a group of marine snails is buried in sediment after dying. By chance, one snail gets buried by coarse sand, another by fine sand, and a third by clay. In your group, discuss the questions on the following page.

Investigating Earth Systems

INVESTIGATING FOSSILS

Inquiry
Hypotheses

A hypothesis is a testable statement or idea about how something works. It is based on what you think that you know or already understand. A hypothesis is never a guess. A hypothesis forms the basis for making a prediction and is used to design an experiment or observation. Guesses can be useful in science, but they are not hypotheses.

- Which sediment size do you think is likely to leave the most detailed impression of each of these items, and why?
- Which would make the least accurate impression, and why?
- Suppose that the snails were moving across the three kinds of sediment before their death. In which sediment is a trace fossil most likely to form? Why?

a) Record the results of your discussion in your journal. These are your predictions. Now you are going to have a chance to test them.

2. Your group will make an impression of a clamshell, a leaf, and a piece of dried fruit, using one of three sediments: coarse sand, fine sand, or clay. Then you will make an impression "fossil."

To share the work, each group will be responsible for one sediment sample. However, each group will test the same items and follow the same procedure.

F 12

Investigating Earth Systems

Investigation 2: Sediment Size and Fossil Formation

Here is the procedure for making impressions:
- Protect the surface of your desk by covering it with newspaper.
- Label a small container with the name of your group.
- Lubricate the insides of the container with petroleum jelly. (The container should be just big enough so that the leaf, the clamshell, and the fruit fit, with minimal extra space.)
- Add 1 cm of sediment (clay, fine sand, or coarse sand) to the container.
- Place each item on the bed of sediment.
- Gently push each item into the sediment. Hold it there for a moment, then carefully remove it and set it aside.
- Mix water with molding plaster or plaster of Paris. Stir and continue adding water until it has the consistency of thin pancake batter.
- Carefully spread an even layer of plaster on top of the imprint.
- Gently tap the sides of your container for one or two minutes. You should see tiny air bubbles come to the surface.
- Let the plaster harden overnight.

3. Carefully remove the plaster from the container, disposing of the sediment as directed by your teacher. Gently rinse and dry the plaster.

   Using a magnifying glass, observe the objects that were used to make the imprint.

   a) Can you see their features in the plaster?

   b) Is there any variation between the objects used to make the impression, and the quality of the impression? Explain.

4. Prepare a display of your impression fossils, labeling the type of sediment used.

5. Observe other groups' impression fossils.

   a) Which sediment type made the most detailed impression?

Investigating Earth Systems

INVESTIGATING FOSSILS

   b) Which sediment type made the least detailed impression?

   c) Give evidence to explain your answers.

   d) Do you accept your original prediction or do you reject it?

6. Discuss the results with the rest of the class.

   a) What generalization can you make about sediment size and its relationship to imprint fossils? Is there agreement among your classmates about this generalization?

   b) What are other kinds of fossils that you know about?

   Do you think that the same relationship between sediment type and fossilization would be seen with other kinds of fossils as well? Explain your answer.

As You Read...
Think about:
1. How are silt, clay, and mud related in terms of sediment size?
2. What are two ways that sediment is formed?
3. In what kind of sedimentary rock are fossils most common? Why?
4. Compare and contrast the formation of a mold fossil and a cast fossil.

Digging Deeper

FOSSILIZATION AND SEDIMENT SIZE
Sediments

Sediment ranges in size from large boulders to very fine mud. Sediments coarser than 2 mm (millimeters) are called gravel. Sand is defined as sediment with sizes between one-sixteenth of a millimeter and 2 mm. All sediment finer than sand is called mud. The coarser part of the mud is called silt, and the finer part is called clay.

Sediments are formed when rocks on the land surface are broken down by rain, wind, and sunlight. Sediments consist of particles of minerals, and also loose pieces of rock. Streams and rivers move the sediments downstream toward the ocean. Some of the sediment is stored in large river valleys, but most of it reaches the ocean. Some is deposited in shallow water near the shore, and some is carried far out into the deep

F 14

Investigating Earth Systems

Investigation 2: Sediment Size and Fossil Formation

ocean. Most of the sediment deposited near the shore is coarse, and it gets finer farther away from the shore. Most of the sediment in the deep ocean is very fine mud.

Sediments are also formed when calcium carbonate minerals are precipitated from warm, shallow waters in the ocean. Much of this is used by marine animals to make their skeletons. After the animals die, their skeletons become sediment. Where currents are weak, this sediment stays where the animals lived. Where currents are strong, the shells are moved along the bottom and are worn into rounded particles.

Fossils in Sedimentary Rocks

In certain conditions, and over a very long period of time, sediment becomes compacted and cemented into sedimentary rock. Fossils are more common in some kinds of sedimentary rocks than others. There are many factors that can contribute to the likelihood of an organism being preserved as a fossil. You investigated one of these, grain size, in this investigation. Fossils are most common in limestones. That is because most limestones consist partly or mostly of the shells of

Investigating Earth Systems

INVESTIGATING FOSSILS

organisms. Sometimes, however, the shells are worn so much that they look like ocean sediment grains rather than "real" fossils. Fossils are also common in shales, which form from muds. As you have already learned, excellent imprint fossils can be formed in fine-grained sediments like muds. Only some shales contain fossils, however, because many areas of muddy ocean floor had conditions that were not suitable for animal life. In this case, only swimming or drifting organisms that die and fall into the mud have a chance to become fossilized. Although this does happen, it is a very rare occurrence. Some sandstones contain fossils as well. Most sandstones do not contain fossils, for various reasons. Water currents in the environment might have been too strong for animals to survive. Also, sands are very porous, so water seeping through the sand might have dissolved the shells away long before the sand was buried and changed into sandstone.

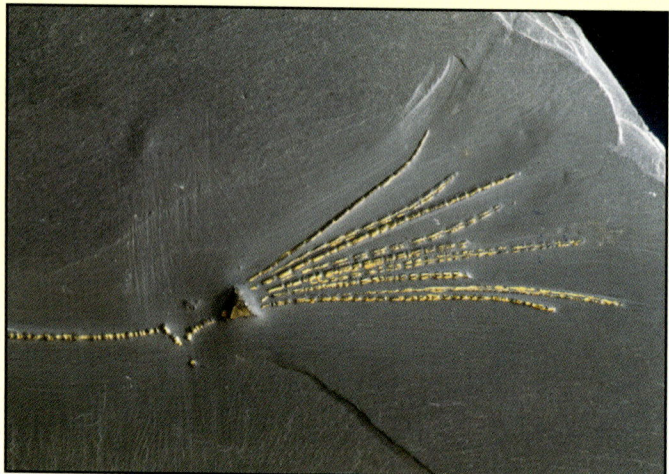

Kinds of Fossils

Sediments are home for many kinds of marine animals. Some animals live on the surface of the sediment, and some burrow into it. Some fossil shells are found mixed with the mud they lived in. Other fossil shells were

Investigation 2: Sediment Size and Fossil Formation

moved by strong currents and deposited along with sand or even gravel. If the shells are buried by more sediment before they are worn away or dissolved, they become fossilized.

Sometimes a fossil consists of original shell material. This is common in very young sediments that have not yet been turned into rock. Older sediments usually have been buried deeply by later sediments and turned into rock. Then it is more likely that the original shell has been dissolved away by water seeping through the pore spaces in the sediment. The fossil is left as an imprint of the original shell. An imprint like that is called a mold. Sometimes the space that was occupied by the shell is now empty. In other cases that space has been filled with later minerals that were precipitated by the flowing pore water. That material, which has the shape of the original shell, is called a cast.

Clams have shells that are in two parts, called valves. The valves are hinged along one edge. They are left and right, like your hands when you put them together along your little fingers. The clam can open its shell to feed and close its shell for protection. Think about what you might see when the clamshell is fossilized. Each valve has an outer surface and an inner surface. Depending on which valve you are seeing, and whether you are seeing the inside or the outside of it, and whether you are seeing its cast or its mold, eight different views are possible! Paleontologists have to be very careful to match up the fossils they see. Otherwise, they might think they are seeing fossils of several different kinds of animal rather than just one.

INVESTIGATING FOSSILS

Review and Reflect

Review

1. Choose several objects from everyday life and compare them to the sizes of gravel, sand, and mud.
2. Give two reasons why fossils are relatively uncommon in sandstones.

Reflect

3. Think back to **Part B** of the investigation. Explain why you think that the clamshell made a better impression in fine-grained sediment than in the coarse-grained sediment.
4. From what you have learned in this investigation, do you think that a sandy beach is a good place for fossils to be preserved? Why or why not?

Thinking about the Earth System

5. Where do sediments come from? Describe any connections that you can make between the hydrosphere, the atmosphere, and the geosphere in the formation of sand and mud deposits. Note these on your *Earth System Connection* sheet.
6. How is the biosphere related to the formation of some sediments? Note any connections between the biosphere and sediment formation on your *Earth System Connection* sheet.

Thinking about Scientific Inquiry

7. How did you use mathematics in this investigation?
8. How did you support a prediction with evidence?
9. Describe how you modeled the process of fossilization in this investigation. In what ways was your model like the natural process of fossilization? In what ways was it different?

Investigation 3: Conditions for Fossil Formation

Investigation 3:
Conditions for Fossil Formation

Key Question

Before you begin, first think about this key question.

Where can fossils form?

In the last activity you discovered that sediment size affects fossilization. Think about what you know about fossil formation. What other factors affect whether or not an organism becomes a fossil?

Share your thinking with others in your group and with your class. Keep a record of the discussion in your journal.

Materials Needed

For this investigation your group will need:
- stream table, or similar setup
- wooden block (or books) to tilt stream table
- dry sand (as fine as possible)
- watering can
- water source
- two tree leaves, pre-soaked in water overnight
- two clamshells
- topographic map of your local area, or physical map of your region
- cardboard
- set of compasses
- scissors
- protractor
- sharpened pencil or dowel

Investigate

Part A: Location, Location

1. With your group, examine your school grounds and, if possible, wooded or moist areas like stream banks, gullies, and along the shores of lakes. You may need to complete this part of the activity on a weekend at home or at a local park, under adult supervision.

Investigating Earth Systems

INVESTIGATING FOSSILS

When examining the school grounds or other areas, you should be supervised by a teacher, parent, or other responsible adult.

Do not handle any living or dead organisms or other litter you find.

Look for living plants and animals like birds, small mammals, and insects. Also look for evidence of death or decay, like leaf litter, carcasses, feathers, and bones. If this is not available, look for human-made litter (i.e., trash).

a) In your journal, keep careful notes about what you observe, and where you observed it. Draw a map of the area and mark on the map where you found the objects.

2. Upon return to the classroom, talk over your observations with your group and with your class.

a) Describe what you observed that indicates decay.

b) Describe what you observed that indicates preservation.

c) Did you find any potential fossils? What were they and why do you think they could become fossils?

d) If most dead organisms can become fossils, would you have expected to find more evidence for this on your outdoor excursion? What does this tell you about the likelihood of something becoming a fossil?

e) What new questions arose from this discussion?

Together, make a class list of key points and questions.

3. You will now build a model that may help you find answers to some of the questions you have generated. In particular, you will model how remains of certain organisms are more likely to be protected from decay than others.

Use a stream table or a large, flat, plastic container about one meter long. Tilt the container by using a book or wooden block at one end.

F
20
Investigating Earth Systems

Investigation 3: Conditions for Fossil Formation

Pour a little water into the lower end, and place a wet leaf and shell underwater on the container floor.

Put a pile of sand on the upper part of the container. Put a leaf and a shell on top of the sand.

4. Predict what will happen if you slowly add water to the upper end of the stream table, as if to model rain.

   a) Record your prediction. Include a reason for your prediction.

5. Slowly and carefully, model heavy rain falling on the land at the upper edge of your model. You may wish to use a watering can to apply the water to the sand.

6. When you have completed your test, observe where the leaves and shells have ended up. Review your predictions and the reasons for them.

   a) Were your predictions correct? Did the results surprise you?

7. Think about the model and your trip outdoors.

   a) In nature, which of the two leaves would be more likely to become a fossil over time, and why?

   b) Which of the two shells would be more likely to become a fossil?

   c) Based on your model, what kind of places would fossils be more likely to form?

8. Look at the diagram and compare it to a topographic map of your local area.

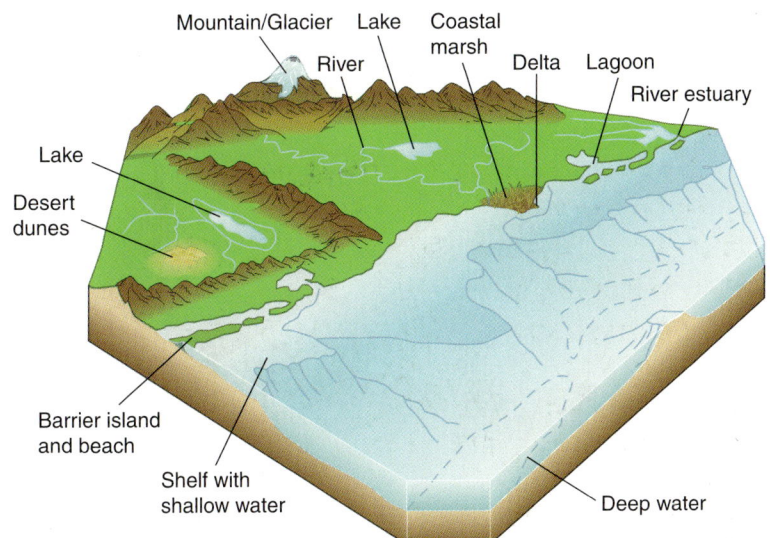

Inquiry
Models

Scientists and engineers use models to help them think about processes that happen too slowly, too quickly, or which cannot be directly observed. Choosing a useful model is one of the instances in which intuition and creativity come into play in science and engineering. In this investigation, you will build a model that will help to identify locations in which an organism is more likely to become fossilized.

Keep in mind that models are imperfect representations of natural processes. They are both like and unlike what they represent, in a number of ways.

Investigating Earth Systems

INVESTIGATING FOSSILS

a) Looking at the diagram, where on the land and under water do you think fossils might have formed in the past? Why?

b) Where do you think there is a chance that fossils might begin to form now?

c) What conditions would be necessary for fossils to begin to form now? What would have to happen?

d) Where do you think you might find conditions that lead to fossil formation in your local area or region?

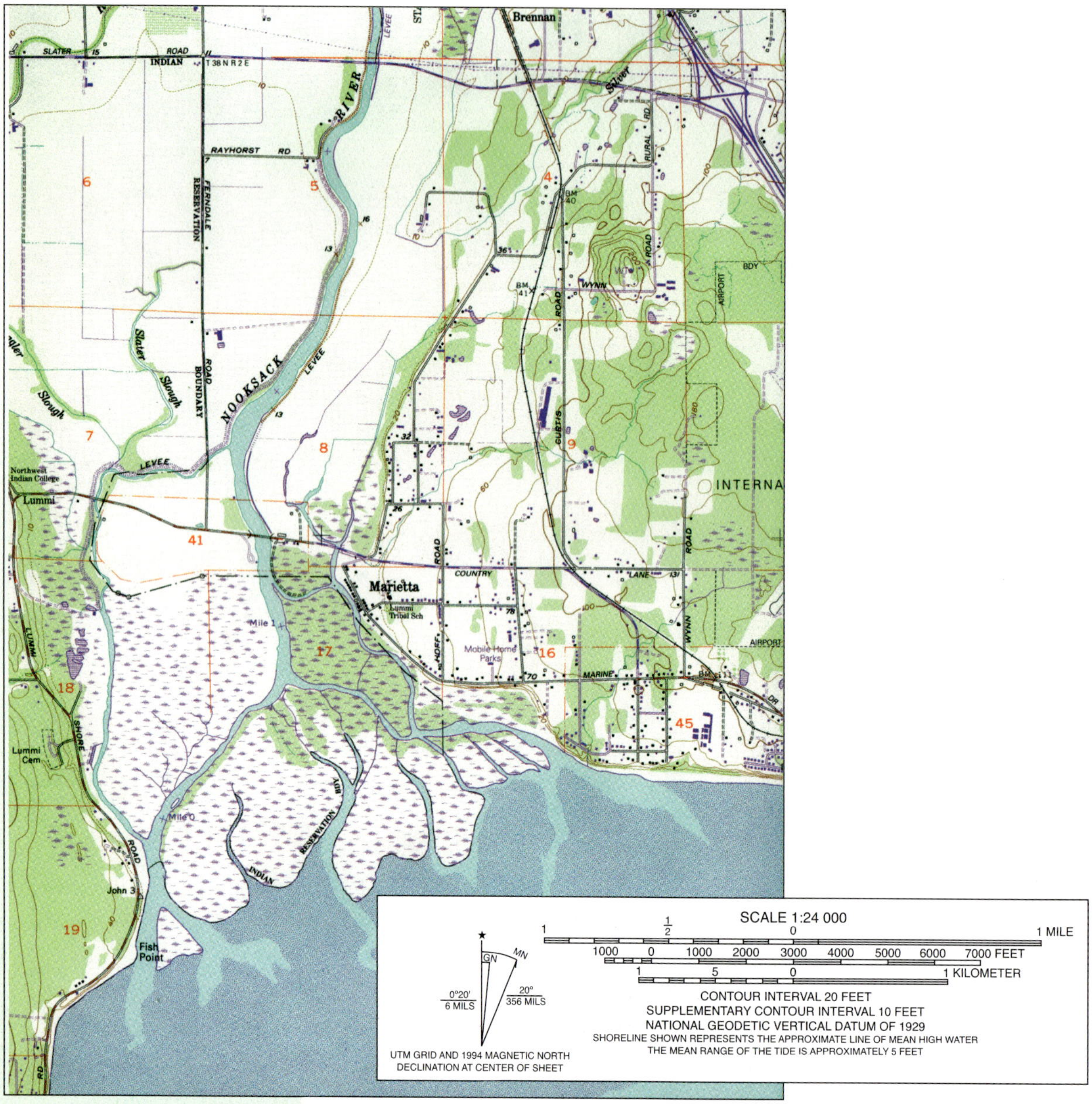

Investigation 3: Conditions for Fossil Formation

9. Test your ideas by conducting research on your local area and/or region.

   a) Did you find that there are fossils in your local area and/or region? Where were the fossils located? Were they abundant in the area that you thought they would be? If not, how do you explain this? Share your findings with your class.

Part B: "Wheel of Fossilization"

1. Imagine that you observe a recently living organism in the ocean.

   a) What might happen to the remains?

   b) Will it leave behind any fossil evidence? Explain why or why not.

2. To investigate the possible fates of different organisms, you will play a game using the "Wheel of Fossilization." First, your group will need to construct a "wheel," similar to the one shown in the diagrams.

   - Construct the wheel by cutting out a circle of cardboard.
   - Divide the circle into 12 roughly equal sections.
   - Number the sections 1-12.
   - Push a pencil through the center.

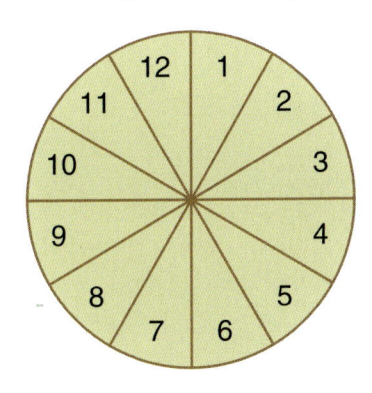

3. You will consider the position of a recently living organism, and the wheel will decide its fate. One of your group members will spin the wheel for you. The fate of the organism is determined by the number touching the desk when it stops spinning.

Investigating Earth Systems

F
23

INVESTIGATING FOSSILS

Possible Fates on the Wheel of Fossilization

1. You are a saber-toothed cat. Your body decomposes and your bones disintegrate in a field—NO FOSSIL
2. You are a shelled protozoan (a foraminiferan). Your body decomposes and your shell dissolves in the deep sea—NO FOSSIL
3. You are an oak tree. Your wood and leaves all decompose in a forest—NO FOSSIL
4. You are a snail. Your shell is preserved as a fossil, but rock erosion later destroys it—NO FOSSIL
5. You are a clam. Your shell is buried by mud in a quiet water setting—YOUR SHELL FOSSILIZES
6. You are a barnacle. Your body and shell are metamorphosed in an undersea lava flow—NO FOSSIL
7. You are a jellyfish. You have no hard skeleton, and your soft body decomposes —NO FOSSIL
8. You are a crab. You get eaten and your shell gets broken down into tiny bits in the process—NO FOSSIL
9. You are a tree fern. Your leaves are buried and preserved in swamp mud—YOUR TISSUES FOSSILIZE
10. You are a clamshell. Your body decomposes and your shell is broken to bits by waves—NO FOSSIL
11. You are a snail shell. Your body decomposes and your shell is recrystallized during mountain-building—NO FOSSIL
12. You are a *Tyrannosaurus rex*. Your footprint in mud is buried by sand along a river—YOUR TRACK FOSSILIZES.

4. Repeat so that each group member has three turns at the "Wheel."

   a) How many members of your group ended up becoming fossils?

   b) Did any one person become a fossil more than once?

   c) What happened to you, according to the fates given by the "Wheel?"

   d) Do you think this is a realistic game? Why or why not?

   Share the results of your group's discussion with the rest of the class.

   e) Keep a record of the discussion in your journal.

Investigation 3: Conditions for Fossil Formation

Digging Deeper

THE LIKELIHOOD OF FOSSILIZATION

For a fossil to form, several conditions have to be met. First of all, the animal had to live in the given area! Animals live in many environments on Earth, but not everywhere. The water above many lake bottoms and some areas of the deep ocean bottom are stagnant. The bottom water is never exchanged with surface waters, so the water contains no dissolved oxygen. Animals cannot live without oxygen, so no animals live there. In these situations, the only possibility of fossilization is if a fish or other swimming or floating animal dies in oxygen-rich waters above, sinks down into the stagnant muddy bottom, and is buried by sediments.

Most environments on the land surface are populated with animals. Fossilization on land is very uncommon, however, because most areas of the land are being eroded. Unless there is deposition, fossils cannot be preserved. Deposition on land is common only in river valleys. Fossils are fairly common in sediments deposited on river floodplains.

Some ocean environments that support animal life are exposed to very strong currents and waves. After a shelled animal dies, the strong water motions cause the hard body parts to be broken and worn. Often the shells end up only as rounded grains of sand or gravel, which no longer look like fossils.

As You Read...
Think about:
1. Why are very few fossils found in rocks made from sediments that are laid down in deep ocean waters? What fossils would you expect to find in these rocks?
2. How does erosion affect the likelihood of fossilization? How does deposition affect the likelihood of fossilization?
3. Under what conditions are soft-bodied animals fossilized?

Investigating Earth Systems
F 25

INVESTIGATING FOSSILS

For animals without skeletons, like worms or jellyfish, fossilization is a very rare event. When paleontologists find a well-preserved fossil of a soft-bodied animal, it's an occasion for celebration. For a soft-bodied animal to be fossilized, its body must be protected from decomposition. The body is usually exposed to air and water with a lot of oxygen, so it decomposes rapidly. The animal is likely to be fossilized only if it is buried soon after it dies (or when it is buried alive!). Even then, it is likely to decompose, because water that seeps through the sediment around it usually is rich in oxygen. Sometimes, however, the body is buried rapidly by fine mud. Water seeps through mud much more slowly than through sand, so the body does not decompose as fast. Mud often contains a lot of other organic matter as well, and that uses up oxygen faster. Some animal bodies then escape decomposition. Under just the right conditions, a delicate impression of the animal might be preserved.

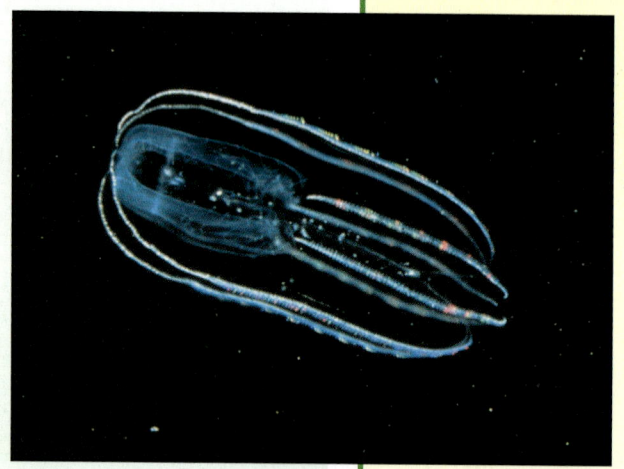

Paleontologists are sure that the fossil record is biased. That means that some kinds of organisms are much scarcer as fossils than they were when they were alive. Other kinds of organisms are much better represented by fossils. Animals with hard shells and skeletons are represented well in the fossil record. On the other hand, soft-bodied animals are probably represented very poorly. It's likely that most soft-bodied species that ever existed are gone forever without a trace. Land animals are probably very poorly represented as well. For example, most animals that are now alive, or have ever lived, are insects, but the fossil record of insects is poor.

Investigation 3: Conditions for Fossil Formation

Review and Reflect

Review

1. a) Why are low-lying areas more likely to accumulate fossils?

   b) Why is this not always true?

2. What are some factors that determine if a recently living organism ends up fossilized?

Reflect

3. Would you expect animals that lived in the oceans near a river delta to be better represented in the fossil record than animals that lived on land? Why or why not?

4. Would you be more likely to find a fossil of a freshwater fish or a hyena? Explain your reasoning.

5. Earth's earliest life was microscopic and soft-bodied. What challenges does this present for scientists who study early life on Earth?

6. What does it mean that the fossil record is biased? What causes it to be biased?

Thinking about the Earth System

7. On your *Earth System Connection* sheet, note how the things you learned in this investigation connect to the geosphere, hydrosphere, atmosphere, and biosphere.

8. What are some advantages and disadvantages of using the geosphere to understand the biosphere of the past?

Thinking about Scientific Inquiry

9. Scientists use evidence to develop ideas. What evidence do you have that becoming a fossil is rare?

10. How did you use a model in this investigation to investigate fossilization? How could you modify the model to make it more realistic?

Investigating Earth Systems

INVESTIGATING FOSSILS

Investigation 4:

Fossils through Geologic Time

Key Question
Before you begin, first think about this key question.

How can we determine the age of a fossil?

Think about what you know about the conditions under which fossils form. If different fossils are found in different layers of rock, could you tell which fossils are the oldest? The youngest?

Share your thinking with others in your class. Keep a record of the discussion in your journal.

Materials Needed
For this investigation your group will need:
- metric measuring tape (as long as possible)
- chalk
- chart paper
- calculator
- "stratigraphic" notebook with "fossils" (this can be made using the detailed instructions provided in the Teacher's Edition)

Investigate

Part A: Geologic Time

1. Geologists know that Earth is about 4.5 billion (4,500,000,000) years old. Primitive life evolved as much as 3.5 billion years ago, or more, but large and complicated life did not develop until much later. In terms of Earth's history, humans are very recent. Find them on the chart.

Investigation 4: Fossils through Geologic Time

a) When did modern humans appear?

b) How does this compare to when life began on the planet?

2. To get a better sense of this kind of time scale, your group is going to think of time as if it were distance.

In a suitable place (a corridor or the schoolyard), mark a starting point with chalk. Next, each person should walk 10 normal paces, mark the distance with chalk, and put his or her name beside this point.

Major Divisions of Geologic Time
(boundaries in millions of years before present)

Era	Period	Event	
Cenozoic	Quaternary	modern humans	
			1.8
	Tertiary	abundant mammals	
			65
Mesozoic	Cretaceous	flowering plants; dinosaur and ammonoid extinctions	
			145
	Jurassic	first birds and mammals; abundant dinosaurs	
			213
	Triassic	abundant coniferous trees	
			248
Paleozoic	Permian	extinction of trilobites and other marine animals	
			286
	Pennsylvanian	fern forests; abundant insects; first reptiles	
			325
	Mississippian	sharks; large primitive trees	
			360
	Devonian	amphibians and ammonoids	
			410
	Silurian	early plants and animals on land	
			440
	Ordovician	first fish	
			505
	Cambrian	abundant marine invertebrates; trilobites dominant	
			544
Proterozoic		primitive aquatic plants	
			2500
Archean		oldest fossils; bacteria and algae	

⚠ Check for any hazards before pacing off your steps.

Investigating Earth Systems

F
29

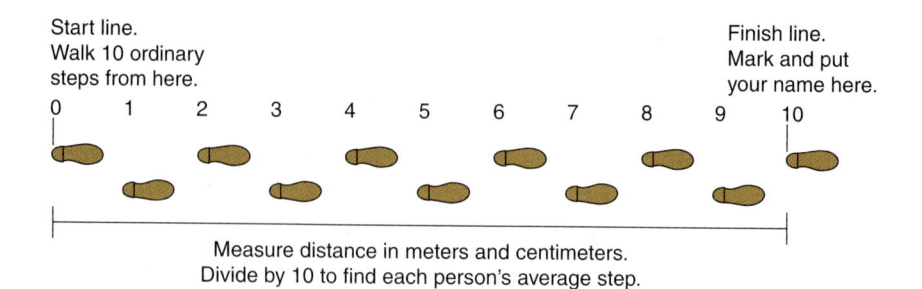

INVESTIGATING FOSSILS

Start line.
Walk 10 ordinary steps from here.

Finish line.
Mark and put your name here.

0　1　2　3　4　5　6　7　8　9　10

Measure distance in meters and centimeters.
Divide by 10 to find each person's average step.

3. When everyone in your group has measured his or her 10-step distance, put the lengths on a chart like the one shown.

Names of Group Members	Distance of Steps (in meters and centimeters)	Average Step (total distance for each person divided by 10)
Total for Your Group (add each person's average)		T =
Average Group Step (divide total by number of persons in your group)		AGS =

4. Find the Average Class Step (ACS) by taking the Total (T) for each group, adding them all together, and dividing the total figure by the number of students participating. How does this number compare to the Average Group Step (AGS)?

   You may want to round the ACS figure up or down to make it into the nearest convenient number (for example, if it is 78 cm, round it up to 80 cm).

5. You will now apply your average distance to time.

   Think of one average step as representing 100 years of time. On this scale it means:

   - You have lived for about one-eighth of a step.
   - Your parents have probably lived for about one-third of a step.
   - Only someone at least 100 years old would have lived one step or more.

Investigating Earth Systems

Investigation 4: Fossils through Geologic Time

Look again at the Major Divisions of Geologic Time chart.

In your group, figure out how many steps would represent life through time for the beginning of each of the periods starting with the Cambrian Period, when a great many different kinds of animals become common in the fossil record. How many steps would be required to represent all of the time that life has been on Earth (about 3.5 billion years)?

6. To get another sense of the huge scale of geologic time, use some mathematical calculations. Imagine that you want to make a movie that will include life through time starting from the origin of the Earth to today. Suppose this movie is going to be 24-h long!

   a) How long would humans be on the screen?

   Share your answer, and the calculations you used to get it, with the rest of the class.

Part B: Life through Geologic Time

1. On a long gymnasium floor, a corridor, or a parking lot, measure out a distance of at least 100 ft (about 30 m).

   Use a 100-foot tape measure or lay out a 100-foot piece of rope between the beginning and end of that distance. This will represent all of geologic time.

2. Your teacher will give you a chart that shows the dates when various kinds of animals first appeared in the fossil record. Plot these dates along the line. To do that, you will have to form a ratio. For each kind of animal, divide the date of appearance by the total length of geologic time. Use that ratio to figure out where to put the point along your 100-foot line. If you are not sure how to do this, your teacher will help you.

   a) Where would a point be that stands for your age?

   b) Where would a point be that stands for your grandparent's age?

   c) Where would a point be that stands for the beginning of recorded human history (about 4000 years)? How does that compare with the time since the dinosaurs became extinct?

Investigating Earth Systems

F
31

INVESTIGATING FOSSILS

Part C: Figuring out the Fossil Record

1. Your teacher will give each group a special notebook. Think of the notebook as a sequence of sedimentary rock layers. Geologists call this a stratigraphic section. You might see such a section in a highway cut, a river bank, or a sea cliff. Each page stands for a single layer in the sequence.

   Each notebook comes from some place around the world. Each one is different. The number of layers is not the same from notebook to notebook, and the layers themselves are different.

   Some of the layers contain fossils. Some do not. The names of the different fossils are shown by capital letters on the pages. These letters have nothing to do with the age of the fossils.

   You need to keep three important things in mind.

   - Sedimentary rock layers are originally deposited one on top of another in horizontal layers. The oldest layer is at the bottom of the stack, and the youngest is at the top.

     The first part of this statement (that sedimentary rock layers are deposited one on top of another) is called the "Law of Superposition."

     The second part of the statement (about originally being in horizontal layers) is called the "Law of Original Horizontality."

     Combined, these two ideas are very important, because they provide a means to tell which rock layers (and fossils in those rock layers) are older than others.

   - Different kinds of plants and animals are called species. A species appears at a certain time and most become extinct at a later time. Once a species becomes extinct, it never appears again.

Inquiry
Laws in Science

In science and nature, the word "law" is given a very special status. A scientific law or a law of nature is generally accepted to be true and universal. Laws are accepted at face value because they have been so strongly tested, and yet have always been observed to be true. A law can begin as a hypothesis, but only after years and even decades of testing can a hypothesis become a law. It can become a law only if it has been shown to be true over and over again, without exception. A law can sometimes be expressed in terms of a single mathematical equation, but laws don't always need to have complex mathematical proofs.

Investigating Earth Systems

Investigation 4: Fossils through Geologic Time

- Geologists didn't know beforehand the succession of fossil species through geologic time. They had to figure that out from the succession of fossils in stratigraphic sections all around the world. You're going to do the same thing in this investigation.

2. You will use the data from each group's notebook to figure out the succession of fossil species. Each group has a sheet of poster board with blank columns (one for each group). On each sheet of poster board, plot your succession of layers in one of the columns. In the column, show the contacts between the layers with horizontal lines. If a layer contains one or more kinds of fossils, label them in the column.

Inquiry
Reporting Findings

In this investigation you are mirroring what paleontologists do. Findings are reported by many different paleontologists and are added to the fossil record.

Group 1   Group 2   Group 3   Group 4   Group 5   Group 6

Investigating Earth Systems

INVESTIGATING FOSSILS

3. The time interval when one or more species existed is called a zone. Your job is to figure out the "standard" succession of zones, worldwide. To help you do this, draw light pencil lines between the columns, to match up times when fossils A to Z lived. Erase lines and change them as needed.

4. When you are satisfied that you have figured out the succession, write it down in a vertical column on a blank sheet of paper, with the oldest at the bottom and the youngest at the top.

5. As a class, compare the succession of fossil zones from all of the groups.

   a) Are each group's results the same? If not, discuss the reasons why. Then agree on the single acceptable succession.

   b) Why do some layers contain fossils but other layers have no fossils?

   c) There are two basic reasons why a particular fossil zone might be missing from one or more of the columns. What are these reasons?

   d) How would you use the results of this investigation to tell the ages of the rock layers in a new stratigraphic section?

   e) Imagine that you are studying a newly discovered stratigraphic section somewhere in the world. You find an entirely new fossil species in one of the layers. Would that change your thinking about the standard succession of fossil zones? If not, why not? If so, how?

Investigation 4: Fossils through Geologic Time

Digging Deeper

TELLING GEOLOGIC TIME
Species

Every plant or animal belongs to a species. A species is a population of plants or animals that can breed to produce offspring that can then produce offspring themselves.

Biologists believe that new species evolve from existing species by a process called natural selection. Here's how it works. Genes are chemical structures in the cells of the organism. The nature of the organism is determined by its genes. The organism inherits the genes from its parents. Occasionally, a gene changes accidentally. That's called a mutation. The changed gene is passed on to the next generation. Most mutations are bad, some are neutral but some mutations make the organism more successful in its life. Organisms that inherit that favorable new gene are likely to become more abundant than others of the species.

Sometimes the population of a species becomes separated into two areas, by geography or by climate. Then the two groups no longer breed with each other. The two groups then slowly change by natural selection. Each group changes in different ways. Eventually, the two groups are so different that they can't breed to produce offspring any more. They have become two different species.

As You Read...
Think about:
1. What is a species?
2. How do species change through time?
3. What are index fossils? How are they used in stratigraphic correlations?
4. How has radioactivity been used to refine the geologic time scale?

Investigating Earth Systems

INVESTIGATING FOSSILS

Species eventually become extinct. That means that the population gets smaller and smaller, until no more organisms of that species are left alive. Species become extinct for various reasons. If the environment changes too fast, the species might not be able to adapt fast enough. Also, a new species might evolve to compete with an existing species. Biologists are sure that once a species becomes extinct it never appears again.

In the modern world, biologists can identify species by seeing whether the organisms can breed with one another. Paleontologists have much more trouble with fossil species, because the organisms are no longer around to breed! All that can be done is to match up shells or imprints that look almost identical and then assume that they represent a species. The features of an organism are controlled by its genetics. Thus, similar-looking fossil organisms had similar genetic composition.

The Fossil Record

Paleontologists want to know the history of evolution and extinction of fossil species through geologic time. To do that, they try to study all of the fossils that have been preserved in sedimentary rocks. That's called the fossil record. Paleontologists have been collecting fossils from sedimentary rock layers around the world for

Investigation 4: Fossils through Geologic Time

over 200 years. Their goal is to figure out the succession of species through all of geologic time. Once that succession is known, it serves as a scale of geologic time. Then, if you find a particular fossil in a rock, you know where that rock fits into the geologic time scale.

Cambrian trilobites   Ordovician trilobites   Devonian trilobites

There's a big problem in figuring out the succession of species through geologic time. You ran into this problem in the investigation. You don't know beforehand what the succession of species is! All you have are many stacks of sedimentary rocks (called stratigraphic sections) around the world to look at. No single stack spans all of geologic time, and no single stack has nearly all of the species that ever lived. You have to compare all of the stacks against one another to get the best approximation to the real succession. That's what you did in **Part C** of this investigation. You compared all of the stacks to one another and matched them up to figure out the succession of fossils. Paleontologists are still refining their ideas about the succession, as new fossils are found.

Stratigraphic Correlation

As you probably figured out already, matching up stratigraphic sections from around the world can be very difficult. If there were no fossils and you could only use the characteristics of the rock layers it would be even harder! This is because at any given time, very

INVESTIGATING FOSSILS

different types of sediments can be deposited in different places. It is these sediments that will eventually become the sedimentary rock layers making up the stratigraphic sections. At any given time, mud may be slowly collecting in some places while in other places sand is piling up rapidly. In other places, maybe there is nothing collecting at all! So you see, very different looking rock layers may mark the same time interval in different stratigraphic sections. The process of matching up equivalent "time layers" of rocks in different places is called stratigraphic correlation. One of the best (and oldest) tools for correlating strata around the world is the use of special fossils called index fossils.

Index fossils have two important characteristics. First, they must have been widely distributed around the world. Second, they must have existed for only relatively short periods of geologic time before becoming extinct. Consider a fossil of an organism that lived only in one place, or that existed for very long periods of geologic time. It would be of little use in matching up layers of rock that were deposited far from one another over the same limited span of time.

Dating Rocks

Knowing the fossil record lets a geoscientist place a particular fossiliferous rock layer into the scale of geologic time. But the time scale given by fossils is only a relative scale, because it does not give the age of the rock in years, only its age relative to other layers. Long after the relative time scale was worked out from fossils, geologists developed methods for finding the absolute ages of rocks, in years before the present. These methods involve radioactivity. Here's how one of the important ones works.

Investigation 4: Fossils through Geologic Time

Some minerals contain atoms of the radioactive chemical element uranium. Now and then, an atom of uranium self-destructs to form an atom of lead. Scientists know the rate of self-destruction. They grind up a rock to collect tiny grains of minerals that started out containing some uranium but no lead. Then they use a very sensitive instrument, called a mass spectrometer, to measure how much of the uranium has been changed to lead. Using some simple mathematics, they can figure out how long ago the mineral first formed. Rocks as old as four billion years can be dated this way.

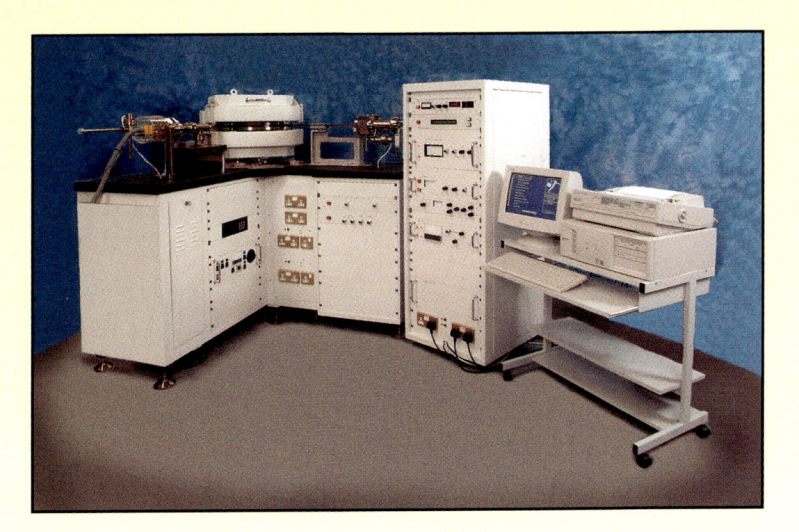

Absolute dating of rocks has provided many "tie points" for the relative time scale developed from fossils. The result is an absolute time scale. When you collect a fossil from a rock, you can place it in the relative time scale. Then you also know about how old it is in years (or usually millions, or tens of millions, or hundreds of millions of years). Even though modern technology makes it possible to date some rocks, the relative time scale is still very important. This is because it takes a lot of time and money to obtain an absolute date, and most rocks cannot be dated using radioactivity.

INVESTIGATING FOSSILS

Review and Reflect

Review

1. According to the chart in this investigation, how long have modern humans (*Homo sapiens*) been on Earth?
2. How are fossils used to match or correlate rock layers deposited in different places at the same time?
3. Why do geologists not use the characteristics of the rocks themselves to identify different rock layers that were deposited at the same time?

Reflect

4. In your own words, explain why you think that geologists still find the relative time scale to be a very useful tool.
5. Why is it that a scientist must look in many places to determine the succession of fossil species through geologic time?

Thinking about the Earth System

6. On your *Earth System Connection* sheet, note how the things you learned in this investigation connect to the geosphere, hydrosphere, atmosphere and biosphere.

Thinking about Scientific Inquiry

7. How did you model the fossil record?

Investigation 5: Comparing Fossils over Time

Investigation 5:

Comparing Fossils over Time

Key Question

Before you begin, first think about this key question.

How are modern organisms different from ancient organisms?

Think about the age of the Earth. How has life changed since the first organisms appeared?

Share your thinking with others in your class. Keep a record of the discussion in your journal.

Materials Needed

For this investigation your group will need:

- fossil clamshell
- hand lens
- eight index cards
- metric ruler or tape measure
- pencil and other drawing implements
- paper clip or a stapler
- fresh clamshells (with clam removed)

Investigate

1. Each group will receive a fossil clamshell.

   Observe the fossil in detail, noting all its characteristics. Remember to observe it from all angles, both inside and out. Each group will have a fossil clamshell. At first glance, they all look very similar. If you look closely, however, you will see fine differences.

Investigating Earth Systems

F
41

INVESTIGATING FOSSILS

Think about any measurements you could make of the fossil clamshell.

Look for any distinguishing features.

Are there any parts or markings that you can use to help you recognize your fossil clamshell among other fossil clamshells?

Pay attention to size and shape. Take lots of measurements. Look for places where muscles might have been attached, where feeding organs may have protruded from the shell, how the animal moved, and any other aspects of "living" that you can suggest.

2. Obtain four index cards.

On one index card, describe the fossil as if you were sending the description to someone who had never seen it before. Include all the observations and any measurements you have made.

Investigation 5: Comparing Fossils over Time

On the other three index cards, make as accurate drawings of the fossil as you can, from three different angles.

Outside view of clamshell fossil

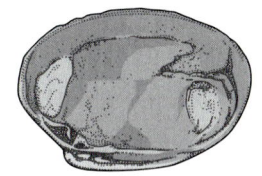

Inside view of clamshell fossil

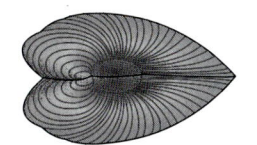

Side view of clamshell fossil

You will need to collaborate on this task. Share the work between your group members. Keep your index cards safe, because you will need them for the next step.

3. All the clam fossils will now be collected, mixed up, and then displayed for all to visit and study. They will be placed in a random order.

   Using your index cards as a guide, try to find your fossil in the collection.

   a) How difficult was it to find your fossil clam? What made it easy or difficult to find?

   b) How accurate were your observations? How accurate is your record of those observations? Do you think that someone else could find your clamshell fossil from your recorded observations? Upon reflection, how would you change your observations and notes to improve them?

4. Fasten your index cards together. Use a paper clip or a staple. Write your names on the top of the first card.

   All the sets of cards will be collected. They will be redistributed so that each group has another group's cards.

   Once again, the clamshell fossils will be displayed, this time in a different order.

   Using the data on the set of index cards you have been given, search and find the clamshell fossil it describes.

   When you think you have identified the clam fossil correctly, check the names of the group members on the first card. Ask that group to verify that you have the correct one.

5. When each group has identified and verified the correct fossil, take time to discuss differences between the clam fossils.

Inquiry
Recording Observations

Scientists are very careful about recording observations. They try not to miss any detail that may turn out to be important later.

They also record their observations in a way that others can see and understand. This will also be important for you to do, because other groups are going to use your records later.

Investigating Earth Systems

INVESTIGATING FOSSILS

Record the results of your discussion in your journal.

a) How are all the clamshell fossils the same? How are they different?

b) What features can be measured, or counted?

c) What characteristics can help to sort one clamshell fossil from another?

d) Make a list of items that could be helpful for future study of clamshells.

This diagram will help you with your observations:

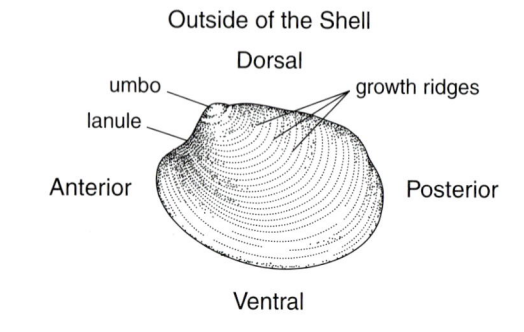

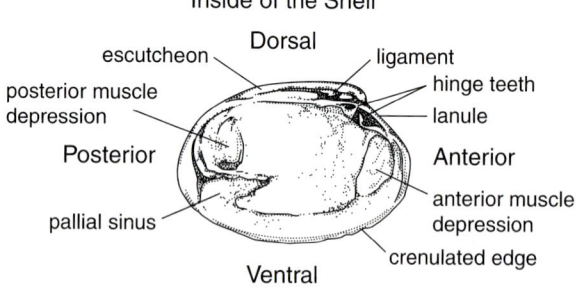

Outside of the Shell
- Dorsal
- umbo
- lanule
- growth ridges
- Anterior
- Posterior
- Ventral

Inside of the Shell
- Dorsal
- escutcheon
- ligament
- hinge teeth
- posterior muscle depression
- lanule
- Posterior
- Anterior
- pallial sinus
- anterior muscle depression
- crenulated edge
- Ventral

6. Your group will now be given a modern clamshell.

Once again, you will use four index cards to make a record of your observations.

You will also repeat the display-and-find process as before, using another group's index-card data to identify their clamshell and verify it.

7. Now, revisit your original fossilized clamshell, and the observations you made on index cards. Lay these alongside the modern clamshell and its set of observations.

Investigation 5: Comparing Fossils over Time

Compare the two. Answer the following questions:

a) How are the two clamshells (ancient and modern) similar? How are they different?

b) Is there any way of telling that one is a fossil and the other is not? If so, how?

c) How can you tell that the fossilized clamshell may be a very ancient relative to the modern clamshell?

Discuss these questions, and any others you think important, first in your group, and then with all other groups. Try to reach an agreement about the similarities and differences between fossil clams and modern clams.

8. By now, you have discovered quite a lot about clams. Spend some time researching them. You will need to use all the resources available to do this.

   The school library can be searched for reference books.

   If you have access to computers, try CD-ROM encyclopedias, or log onto the Internet and search under "clams" (also try "pelecypods" and "bivalves," which are technical terms for clams) for further information.

   a) When your group has completed its research, organize your information in a clear and understandable form. Try to be creative about this. Use any pictures you can find to make your presentation attractive and interesting to others.

   Hold a whole-class session, in which each group shows what it has found out about clamshells.

9. When you have shared all the information you have collected about clams, think about other organisms that have existed through time. Review the Major Divisions of Geologic Time chart on page F29.

   As you do so, discuss and answer these questions:

   a) What other kinds of organisms besides clams have survived for millions of years?

   b) What organisms have become extinct over time?

   c) What might have given some organisms a better chance of survival than others?

   Use any other resources you have available to help find answers to these questions.

Inquiry

Using References as Evidence

When you write a science report, the information you gather from books, magazines, and the Internet comes from scientific investigations. Just as in your investigations, the results can be used as evidence. Because evidence, like an idea, is important, you must always list the source of your evidence. This not only gives credit to the person who wrote the work, but it allows others to examine it and decide for themselves whether or not it makes sense.

INVESTIGATING FOSSILS

As You Read…
Think about:

1. *Why do paleontologists use geometric shape to analyze a collection of fossils?*
2. *According to fossil records, how have organisms evolved during geologic time?*
3. *When did the first multicellular organisms appear in the fossil record?*

Digging Deeper

FOSSILS THROUGH GEOLOGIC TIME
Identifying Fossils

When you sorted fossils by the features of their geometry, you were doing exactly what paleontologists do. A paleontologist collects as many fossils as possible from a rock or sediment. Once the fossils are prepared by scraping and cleaning, they are sorted by geometry. Fossils with very similar geometry are assumed to belong to a single species. That is because an organism's geometry is controlled by its genetics. Fossils with somewhat different geometry are assumed to belong to a different species. Usually, the fossil species has already been studied and named. Sometimes, however, the species is a new one. Then the paleontologist writes a detailed description of the new species, gives the new species a name, and publishes the description for others to read and use in their own work. Not much excites a paleontologist more than discovering a new species!

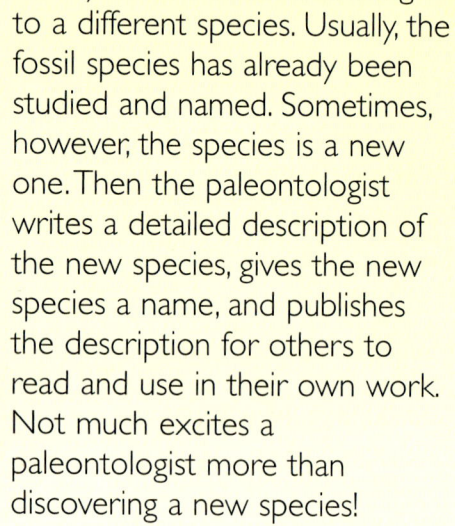

Sorting fossils is tricky business, for several reasons. Some organisms died when they were young and still developing, and some died when they were old. Some were male and some were female. Also, most species show a lot of natural variability. You know that from looking at other members of your own species! It's often impossible for paleontologists to

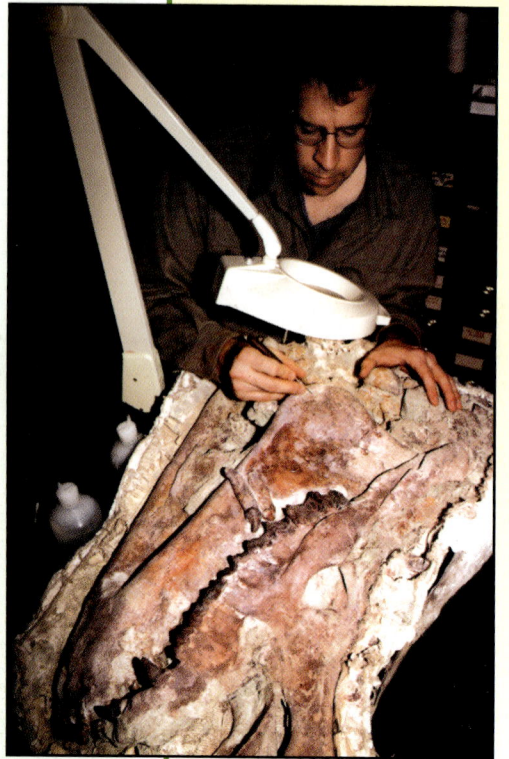

F
46
Investigating Earth Systems

Investigation 5: Comparing Fossils over Time

decide whether they are looking at a single species with a lot of variability, or two similar species.

Evolution in the Fossil Record

The oldest fossils are more than 3.5 billion years old. They are simple unicellular (single-celled) algae, very similar to algae that still exist today. Evolution was very slow until about 700 million years ago, when unicellular organisms with larger and more complex cells evolved. Not long after that, a little more than half a billion years ago, multicellular (many-celled) organisms appeared. Instead of consisting of just a single cell, multicellular organisms have an enormous number of cells, grouped according to their function. Several kinds of multicellular organisms evolved in a very short time, geologically. Paleontologists still do not understand very well how this happened. Many of these early kinds of multicellular organisms, like clams, snails, and corals, are still abundant today. More complex kind of animals, like reptiles, birds, and mammals, evolved even more recently in geologic time.

INVESTIGATING FOSSILS

Review and Reflect

Review

1. What do fossil clams have in common with modern clams?
2. What kind of organism is the oldest found in the fossil record?

Reflect

3. How can you tell that the very ancient clam is related to the modern clam?
4. What are some of the difficulties in identifying fossils?
5. From what you've learned in this investigation, do you think that paleontologists have overestimated or underestimated the number of different species observed in the fossil record? Explain your answer.

Thinking about the Earth System

6. On your *Earth System Connection* sheet, note how the things you learned in this investigation connect to the geosphere, hydrosphere, atmosphere, and biosphere.

Thinking about Scientific Inquiry

7. Why is it important to take good observations?
8. Why is it important in a scientific investigation to record your observations and procedures carefully in a way that is easily understood by others?

Investigation 6: Adaptations to a Changing Environment

Investigation 6:
Adaptations to a Changing Environment

Key Question
Before you begin, first think about this key question.

Why does any given plant or animal look the way it does, and has it always looked that way?

Think about a specific plant or animal and about what characteristics it may have that helps it to survive in this world.

Share your thinking with others in your class. Keep a record of the discussion in your journal.

Materials Needed
For this investigation your group will need:
- gaming die
- poster board
- colored pencils or markers

Investigate
Part A: Building a Better Beast

1. Look at the lists of different types of animal characteristics given on the next page. Each of these characteristics is an adaptation that can

Investigating Earth Systems

F
49

INVESTIGATING FOSSILS

help different animals to survive in the many different habitats on the Earth. For example, ducks have webbed feet to help them swim and dive for food, and they have a layer of down to keep them warm in the water. As a class, discuss some of these characteristics and how they are useful.

Now think about an animal that you may know of or perhaps may have even seen before.

a) What characteristics of that animal help it to adapt to its environment and thrive?

b) Look again at the list of different characteristics given below. Which of those characteristics does your animal have?

c) Share your thinking with your group. As a group, develop a list of animals and their characteristics or adaptations.

Animal Characteristics

| **Eyes**
Forward in head
On sides of head

Feet
Webbed
Clawed
Padded
Hooved

Mouth
Beak
Tearing teeth
Grinding teeth
Cutting teeth | **Covering**
Fur
Feathers
Scales
Skin
Shell

Coloration
Camouflage
Bright

Movement
Running
Flying
Climbing
Swinging
Leaping | **Homes**
Trees
Caves
Underground
Water

When Animals Eat
Day
Night
Dawn or Dusk

Dealing with Heat and Cold
Body Covering
Active/Feeding Times
Homes

Other Defenses
Bad Smell or Taste
Size |

Investigating Earth Systems

Investigation 6: Adaptations to a Changing Environment

2. Look at the two possibilities listed for where the eyes of an animal are in its head. Hypothesize which adaptation you think would be better for a predator to have.

   a) Propose an experiment or study that could test your hypothesis. Write your proposed test down in your journal.

   b) Repeat this same thought process for another of the categories listed. Hypothesize what the advantage for a particular adaptation is and propose a means of testing your hypothesis.

Investigating Earth Systems

F
51

INVESTIGATING FOSSILS

3. It is now your group's job to "build a better beast." Using the table below, roll a die to see what environment your animal will live in.

   Now, roll the die again to see if your animal will be a carnivore (meat eater), a herbivore (plant eater), or an omnivore (both a plant and meat eater).

No.	Habitat	No.	Animal Type
1	open grassland/savanna	1	herbivore
2	tropical rainforest	2	herbivore
3	temperate forest	3	carnivore
4	mountains	4	carnivore
5	desert	5	omnivore
6	wetlands	6	omnivore

4. Work together with your group to design an animal that would have the adaptations necessary to survive given the conditions dictated by your rolls of the dice. To do this, you should first make a list of some of the characteristics of the habitat in which your animal lives.

   You can pick adaptations from the categories listed below. You can also invent your own adaptation.

   a) Draw a picture of your creature and give it a name. Also list each adaptation, and describe how each adaptation will be of benefit to your creature.

5. Participate in a class discussion about each group's animals and adaptations.

Investigation 6: Adaptations to a Changing Environment

Digging Deeper

ADAPTATIONS

Living organisms are adapted to their environment. This means that the way they look, the way they behave, how they are built, or their way of life makes them suited to survive and reproduce in their habitats. For example, giraffes have very long necks so that they can eat tall vegetation, which other animals cannot reach. The eyes of cats are like slits. That makes it possible for the cat's eyes to adjust to both bright light, when the slits are narrow, and to very dim light, when the slits are wide open.

Behavior is also an important adaptation. Animals inherit many kinds of adaptive behavior. In southern Africa there are small animals called meerkats, which live in large colonies. The meerkats take turns standing on their hind legs, looking up at the sky to spot birds of prey. Meanwhile, the meerkats in the rest of the colony go about their lives. You can probably think of many other features of body or behavior that help animals to lead a successful life.

As You Read...
Think about:
1. Describe in your own words what it means that an organism is adapted to its environment.
2. What is an ecological niche?
3. What is a vestigial structure? Provide an example.

Investigating Earth Systems

F
53

INVESTIGATING FOSSILS

In biology, an ecological niche refers to the overall role of a species in its environment. Most environments have many niches. If a niche is "empty" (no organisms are occupying it), new species are likely to evolve to occupy it. This happens by the process of natural selection, which you learned about in **Investigation 4.** By natural selection, the nature of the species gradually changes to become adapted to the niche. If a species becomes very well adapted to its environment, and if the environment does not change, species can exist for a very long time before they become extinct.

The Modern Horse and Some of Its Ancestors

Equus
- Lived from about 5 million years ago to the present
- Lives in areas of the grassy plains
- Eats grasses and is classified as a grazer
- Is about 1.6 m tall at the shoulder
- Has 1 hoofed toe on each of its front and rear limbs.

Merychippus
- Lived from about 17 to 11 million years ago
- Lived in areas with shrubs and on the grassy plains
- Ate leafy vegetation and grasses and is classified as a grazer (the first in the line of horses)
- Was about 1.0 m tall at the shoulder and had a long face and legs making it appear much like a modern horse.
- Had 3 hoofed toes on each of its front and rear limbs. The central toe was much larger than the others.

Miohippus
- Lived from about 32 to 25 million years ago
- Lived in less thickly wooded areas
- Ate leafy vegetation and is classified as a browser
- Was about 0.6 m tall at the shoulder (about the size of a German shepherd dog) and had padded feet.
- Had 3 toes on each of its front and rear limbs.

Hyracotherium-Oldest known horse
- Lived from about 55 to 45 million years ago
- Lived in thickly wooded areas
- Ate leafy vegetation and is classified as a browser
- Was about 0.4 m tall at the shoulder (about the size of a small dog) and had padded feet.
- Had 4 toes on each of its front limbs and three on each of its rear limbs.

Investigation 6: Adaptations to a Changing Environment

Horses are an excellent example of an animal evolving to fill a niche. Many fossils of different kinds of horses have been discovered, and paleontologists think that the earliest ancestor of the modern horse lived in North America more than 50 million years ago. This animal was a small padded-foot forest animal about the size of a dog. If you saw one next to a modern horse, you might not even think the two were related! As time passed, the climate of North America became drier, and the vast forests started to shrink. Grasses were evolving, and the area of grassland was increasing. Horses adapted to fill this new grassland niche. They grew taller, and their legs and feet became better adapted to sprinting in the open grasslands. Their eyes also adapted to be farther back on their heads to help them to see more of the area around them. Each of these adaptations helped the evolving grassland horses to avoid predators. Their teeth also changed to be better adapted to grinding tough grassland vegetation.

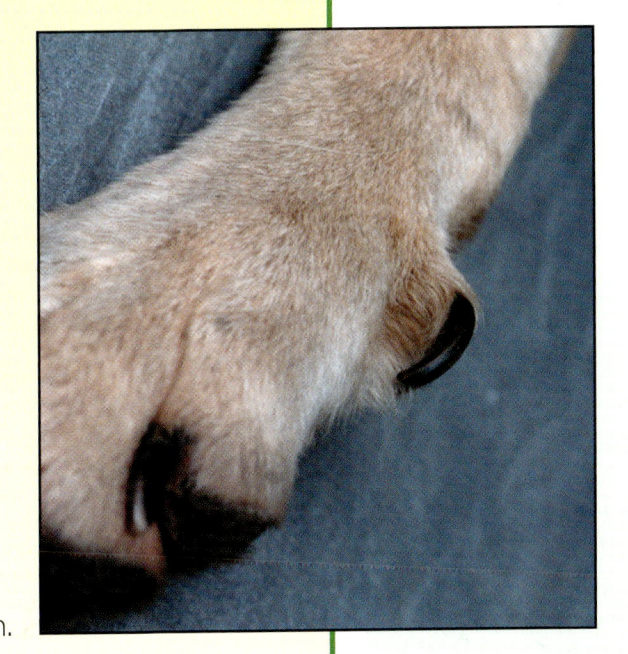

Have you ever wondered what purpose the "dew" claw on the inside of a dog's paw serves? The claw is the dog's thumb. Because a dog runs on the balls of its feet and four digits, the claw no longer serves a purpose. Organs or parts of the body that no longer serve a function are called vestigial structures. They provide evidence that the species is still changing. Even humans have vestigial structures. The human appendix is one such example. It used to store microbes that helped to digest plant matter, but it is no longer needed in the human.

INVESTIGATING FOSSILS

Review and Reflect

Review

1. Are all animal adaptations physical adaptations? Explain your answer.
2. Pick an animal living today and describe two adaptations that help it to survive in its environment.
3. Describe three ways that horses have changed over the past 50 million years.

Reflect

4. Describe how adaptation relates to the process of natural selection that was described in the **Digging Deeper** reading section of **Investigation 4**.
5. What advantage might there be in a predator having soft, padded feet?
6. Examine the diagram on page F29 showing the major divisions of geologic time. How can the concept of ecological niches explain the rapid increase in the number of mammals since the end of the Cretaceous Period?

Thinking about the Earth System

7. What correlation did you make in this investigation between changes in the atmosphere/climate system and changes in the biosphere?

Thinking about Scientific Inquiry

8. How did you use the processes of scientific inquiry in this investigation?

Investigation 7: Being a Paleontologist

Investigation 7:
Being a Paleontologist

Key Question

Before you begin, first think about this key question.

What can fossils tell you about life through time?

Think about what you have learned so far. What kinds of clues can fossils give about Earth history and changing life?

Share your thinking with others in your class. Keep a record of the discussion in your journal.

Materials Needed

For this investigation you will need:

- unknown fossil
- metric ruler and measuring tape
- fossil record charts
- set of known fossil samples
- state or regional geologic map
- access to research material
- materials to create a display

Investigate

1. You will be given an unknown fossil and a geologic map from its state of origin. Examine the fossil carefully.

   a) Write down your first thoughts about it in your journal. Think about these things:
   - What could have made this fossil?

Investigating Earth Systems

INVESTIGATING FOSSILS

- What kind of rock is it in?
- How old might it be?

Inquiry
Using Maps as Scientific Tools

Scientists collect and review data using tools. You may think of tools as only physical objects like shovels and hand lenses. However, forms in which information is gathered and stored are also tools. In this investigation you are using a geologic map as a scientific tool.

You will have the opportunity to conduct research on your fossil, so that you can compare what you think about it now, to what you think about it later on.

2. Using all of your knowledge and resources about fossils, including your geologic map, find out as much as you can about your fossil.

   Later, you can summarize this to give a "portrait" of your fossil sample. This can be in the form of: a model, a poster, a web page, a magazine article, a newspaper article, a brochure, a diorama, a free-standing display, any other method that you choose.

3. Information that you may be able to find out about your fossil should include:

   - what kind of organism it represents;
   - what the organism looked like when it was alive;
   - what parts of the organism were fossilized and what were not (and why);
   - where the organism might have come from originally;
   - what kind of rock the fossil is in;
   - during what time period the fossil organism lived;

Investigation 7: Being a Paleontologist

- detailed description of the fossil itself (dimensions, visual description, texture).

Review the resources that you have in your classroom, in your school, and in your community. Decide what would be the most useful ones, and collect these as you need them.

4. Do your research on your fossil, carefully recording what you find out in your journal, as well as the resources you have used.

5. When you have finished your research, construct your fossil portrait, using one of the methods listed in **Step 2**, or a presentation method of your own.

   Be sure that your portrait covers as many of the questions in **Step 3** as possible.

   Using both pictures and words, make the portrait appealing to your target audience.

6. When all of the fossil portraits are completed, you will have the opportunity to present your work.

   Be prepared to answer questions about your research, the sources of your information, how recent they are, and how reliable they are. Be prepared, also, to ask other students in your class questions about their fossil portraits when they present.

Inquiry

Presenting Information

Scientists are often asked to provide information to the public. In doing so, they need to consider both the information they wish to present and the best method of presenting the information. In this investigation you will need to choose the method of presentation that you think will be the most effective.

Be sure your teacher approves your plan before you begin.

Investigating Earth Systems

INVESTIGATING FOSSILS

As You Read...
Think about:
1. What kind of information does a geological map contain?
2. What is a rock unit?
3. Look at the map and cross section on page F61.
   a) What rock layer is the youngest? Explain your answer.
   b) What rock layer is the oldest? Explain.
   c) How do you know the layers were deformed by pressure?

Digging Deeper

GEOLOGIC MAPS AND CROSS SECTIONS

Geologic maps show the distribution of the solid rock (bedrock) at the Earth's surface. In some places this rock is exposed and in other areas it is buried beneath a thin layer of surface soil or sediment. The number of different kinds of rock in the Earth's crust is enormous. However, the bedrock over a large area is usually the same type. That is because rocks are originally formed in large volumes by a specific process. The rock bodies formed during the same process are called rock units.

A geologic map is more than just a map of rock types. Most geologic maps show the locations and relationships of different rock units. Each rock unit is identified on the map by a symbol of some kind. The symbol is explained in a legend or key, and is often given a distinctive color as well. Part of the legend of a geologic map consists of one or more columns of little rectangles, with appropriate colors and symbols. The rectangles identify the various rock units shown on the map. There is often a very brief description of the units in this part of the legend. The rectangles for the units are arranged in order of decreasing age upward.

Geologic maps show other information as well. They show the symbols that are used to represent such features as folds or faults. They have information about latitude and longitude. They always have a scale, expressed both as a labeled scale bar and as a ratio—1:25,000, for example. The first number is a unit of distance on the map and the second number, after the colon, is the corresponding distance on the actual land surface.

Geologic maps present a general picture of the rock units present. Such generalization is the responsibility of

Investigation 7: Being a Paleontologist

the geologist doing the mapping. The amount of generalization increases as the area covered by the map increases.

Most geologic maps are accompanied by one or more vertical cross sections. These are views of what the geology would look like in an imaginary vertical plane downward from some line on the land surface. The geologist constructs these cross sections after the map is completed. Their locations are selected so as to best reveal the three-dimensional nature of the geology. The degree of certainty about the geology shown on the cross section decreases downward with depth below the surface.

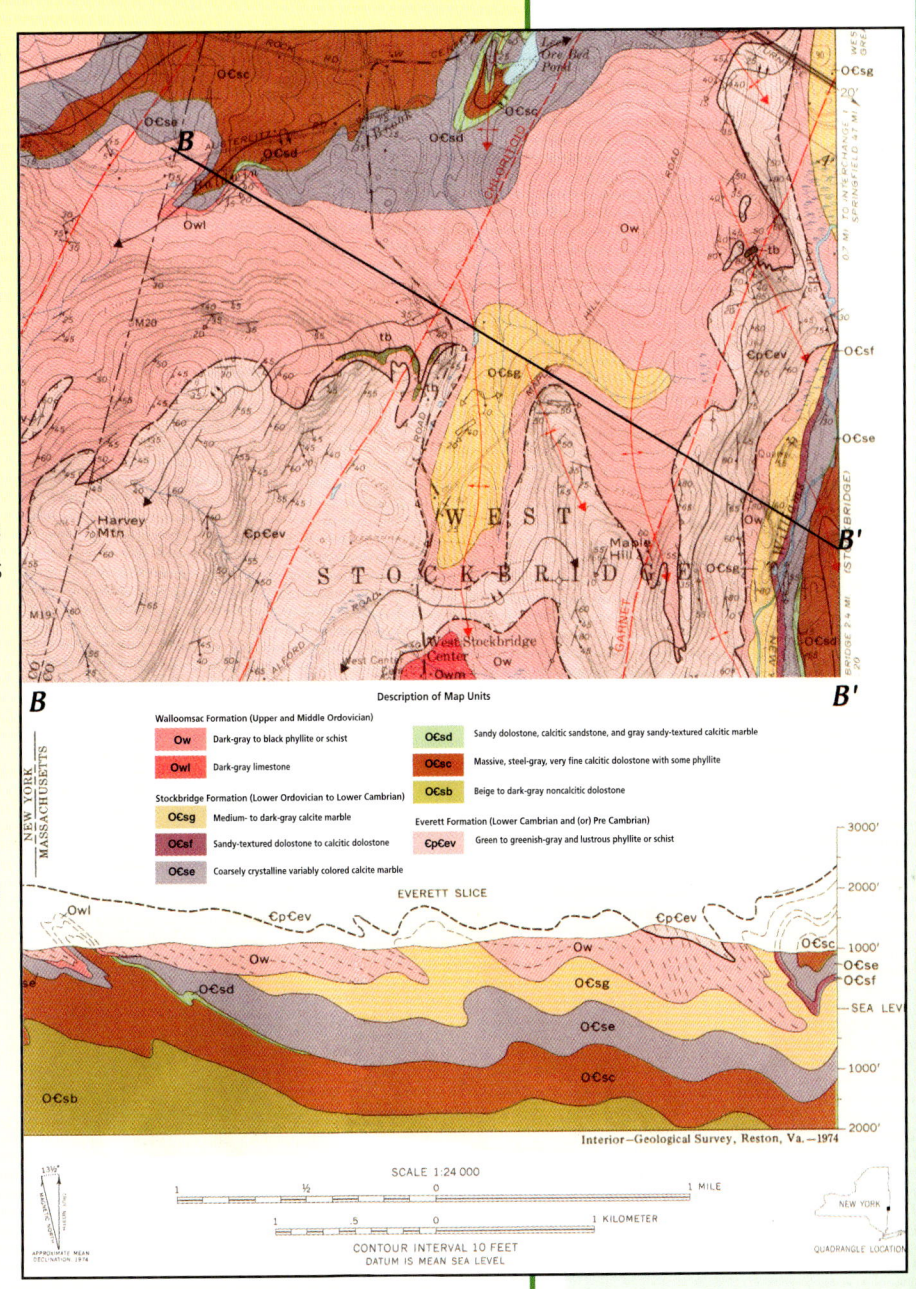

Investigating Earth Systems

INVESTIGATING FOSSILS

Review and Reflect

Review

1. What were the names of the fossils in your classmates' fossil portraits?

Reflect

2. What useful information about fossils could be found on a geologic map?
3. What information on a geologic map could be verified using the fossil record?
4. What have you discovered from this investigation to add to your understanding of life through time?
5. How does the study of fossils help geologists understand life through time?
6. How might understanding Earth's history be useful to humans now and in the future?
7. Think back on the entire research experience with your unknown fossil.
   a) How difficult was it to find the information you wanted?
   b) What resource was most helpful in finding out about your fossil? Why was that?

Thinking about the Earth System

8. How can you use the type of rock that your fossil was in along with information about the fossil animal itself to interpret the environment in which it lived?

Thinking about Scientific Inquiry

9. How did you collect evidence in this investigation?
10. How did you present your findings to others? Why was this important?

Reflecting

Back to the Beginning

You have been studying fossils in many ways. How have your ideas changed since the beginning of the investigation? Look at the following questions and write down your ideas in your journal:

- What is a fossil?
- How are fossils are formed?
- How can we find out how old a fossil is?
- What can fossils tell you about how life changed through time?
- What are some things that you want to understand better about fossils and changes in life through time?

How has your thinking about fossils changed?

Thinking about the Earth System

Consider what you have learned about the Earth system. Refer to the *Earth System Connection* sheet that you have been building up throughout this module.

- What connections between fossils and the Earth system have you been able to find?

Thinking about Scientific Inquiry

You have used inquiry processes throughout the module. Review the investigations you have done and the inquiry processes you have used.

- What scientific inquiry processes did you use?
- How did scientific inquiry processes help you learn about fossils?

A New Beginning

Not so much an ending as a new beginning!

This investigation into fossils is now completed. However, this is not the end of the story. You will see the importance of fossils where you live, and everywhere you travel. Be alert for opportunities to observe the importance of fossils and add to your understanding.

INVESTIGATING FOSSILS

The Big Picture

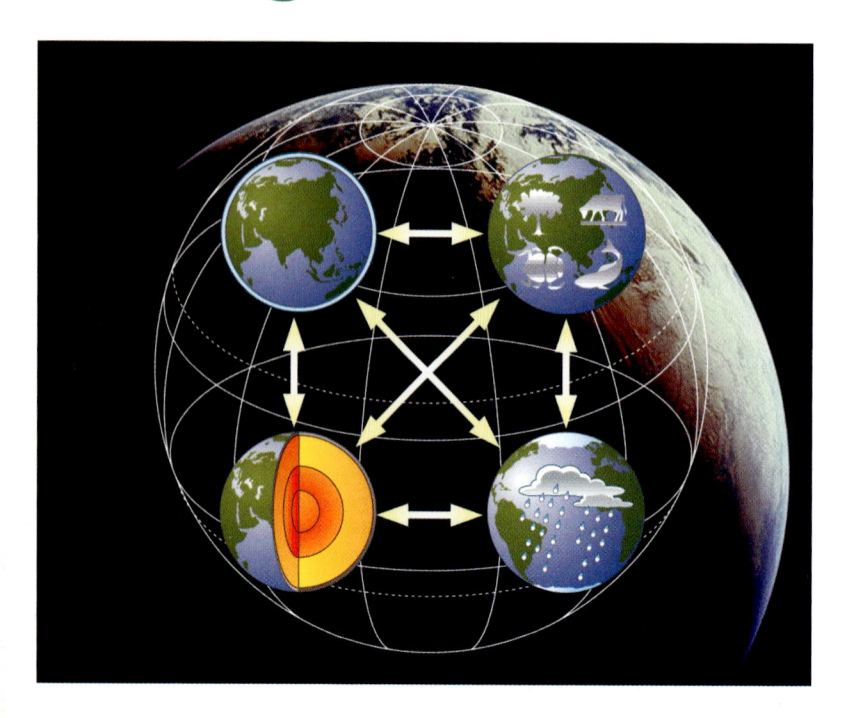

Key Concepts

Earth is a set of closely linked systems.

Earth's processes are powered by two sources: the Sun, and Earth's own inner heat.

The geology of Earth is dynamic, and has evolved over 4.5 billion years.

The geological evolution of Earth has left a record of its history that geoscientists interpret.

We depend upon Earth's resources—both mined and grown.

Glossary

Absolute time scale–The scale of geologic time, measured in years.
Adaptation–A change in a plant or animal species, by the process of natural selection, that makes the species more successful in its environment.
Anaerobic bacteria–Bacteria that are able to live in an environment without oxygen.
Analogy–A correspondence or similarity between two things that otherwise are not exactly the same.
Atmosphere–The layer of gas that surrounds the Earth. The atmosphere is a mixture of several gases.

Biosphere–The part of the Earth System that includes all living organisms (animals and plants) and also dead and decaying plant matter.
Body fossil–A fossil that consists of the preserved body of an animal or plant or an imprint of the body.

Cast–Mineral material that fills a hole that was left when a fossil shell dissolved.
Controlled test–A test, or experiment, in which all other variables are held constant except for one.

Data–Observations, both quantitative and qualitative, from which conclusions can be inferred.
Decomposition–The chemical change when the material of a dead animal or plant or animal decays.
Dependent variable–In an experiment, a variable that is determined by the values of the independent variables that are imposed by the researcher.
Deposition–The process of settling of sediment particles onto a sediment surface beneath water or air; also, the process of precipitation of sedimentary minerals from a body of water.

Earth System–A term used to describe the Earth as a set of closely interacting systems, including all subsystems, like the geosphere, atmosphere, hydrosphere, and biosphere.
Ecological niche–A kind of place or site where there is a particular combination of conditions needed for a species of animal or plant to live.

Erosion–Removal of soil or sediment from a surface by wind or running water.
Estimate–A mathematical approximation.
Evolution–The development of new species of animals or plants from existing species by biological processes like natural selection.
Extinction–The disappearance of a species of animal or plant when all of the members of that species die without reproducing.

Fault–A fracture through rock, along which the masses of rock on either side of the fracture move relative to one another.
Fold–A wavelike structure in a body of rock, caused by forces within the Earth.
Fossil–Any evidence of past life preserved in sediments or rocks.
Fossil record–All of the evidence of past life that is preserved in the rocks of the Earth.

Genes–The chemical units in organisms that transmit heredity from one generation to the next.
Geologic cross section–A diagram that shows rock units and their geological structures on a vertical plane downward from the land surface.
Geologic maps–Maps that show the arrangement of rock units and rock structures on the land surface.
Geologic time scale–The scale of time through Earth history, arranged in terms of officially defined units.
Geologist (or geoscientist)–A person who is trained in and works in any of the geological sciences.
Geology–The study of planet Earth: the materials of which it is made, the processes that act on these materials, the products formed, and the history of the planet and all its life forms since its origin.
Geosphere–The part of the Earth System that includes the crust, mantle, and inner and outer core.

Habitat–The place where an animal or plant species lives and grows.
Hydrosphere–The part of the Earth system that includes all the planet's water, including oceans, lakes, rivers, groundwater, ice, and water vapor.

Investigating Earth Systems

INVESTIGATING FOSSILS

Hypothesis–A statement that can be proved or disproved by experimental or observational evidence; a scientist's best estimation, based on scientific knowledge and assumptions of the results of an experiment.

Independent variable–In an experiment, a variable which can be controlled by the researcher and which determines the values of other variables (called dependent variables).

Inquiry–The process of finding answers to questions through a variety of methods. These can include research, fair testing, using models, asking experts, or many other methods.

Law of Original Horizontally–The principle that sediments are usually deposited on a horizontal surface.

Law of Superposition–The principle that younger sediments are usually deposited upon older sediments.

Limestone–A sedimentary rock that consists mostly of a calcium carbonate mineral, usually the mineral calcite.

Model–A representation of a process, system, or object that is too big, too small, too unwieldy, or too unsafe to test directly.

Mold–An impression made in sediment or rock by the outer surface of a fossil shell.

Multicellular organism–An organism that consists of a large number of specialized cells.

Mutation–A permanent change in one or more of the genes of a plant or animal, resulting in offspring that are unlike the parents.

Observations–Data collected using the senses.

Organic compounds–Chemical compounds that consist of atoms of carbon bonded to one another and to atoms of other elements like hydrogen or oxygen.

Paleontologist–A scientist who studies past life.

Paleontology–The study of past life.

Precipitate–A solid chemical substance that is formed by growth from materials dissolved in water.

Radioactive element–A chemical element whose atoms occasionally change into atoms of other chemical elements, giving off energy in the process.

Record–To make a note of observations and events. Recording can be done on paper, electronically, or through other means of communication like video, sound recording, or photography.

Relative time scale–The scale of geologic time expressed in terms of officially defined units but without reference to the age of the units in years.

Sandstone–A sedimentary rock that consists of particles of sand that are cemented together to form a solid rock.

Scientific processes–The methods used by scientists to investigate questions, record data, and analyze results.

Sediment–Particles of minerals and rocks that are transported along the Earth's surface and then deposited.

Sedimentary rocks–Rocks that consist of sedimentary materials.

Species–A group of animals or plants that are capable of producing offspring, that themselves can reproduce.

Stratigraphic correlation–The process of establishing the time equivalence of rocks that exist in areas that are far apart.

Stratigraphic section–A stack or sequence of sedimentary rock layers that are exposed at a given place on the Earth.

Trace fossil–Any evidence of the life activities of a plant or animal that lived in the geologic past (but not including the fossil organism itself).

Unicellular organism–A plant or animal that consists of only a single cell.

Variables–The things about an experiment that can be changed by the researcher.

Verify–To check and confirm data for its reliability. In science, this means that someone checks your procedures and findings.

Vestigial structures–Organs or structures in an organism that once served a purpose earlier in the history of the species, but now have no useful function.